"Philip Sheldrake h
account of mysticis   ht
and practice and as a dynamic part of everyday life. Intelligent,
accessible, and compassionate, *A World Transfigured* illuminates
what it means to live from a deeper ground and why it matters.
A beautiful, profound, and important book."

— Douglas E. Christie, PhD, Professor of Theological Studies,
    Loyola Marymount University, Los Angeles

"*A World Transfigured* is a stunning work: a deeply informed
and quite moving exploration of the origins, interpretations,
and practitioners of 'mysticism.' As a seasoned scholar, Philip
Sheldrake can be counted on to gather together, in a particularly
lucid manner, the vast and complex scholarship on whatever
subject he tackles, wrestling deftly with all vexing questions.
At the same time, he manages to lure us into the depths of the
human spirit in its various faith expressions as it continues its
never-ending journey of desire beyond what can be known."

— Wendy M. Wright, PhD, Professor Emerita of Theology,
    Creighton University

"Mysticism and language have always been complex partners.
In his newest book, Philip Sheldrake manages the difficult task
of helping these sometimes chaotic partners dance together
beautifully. Speaking directly to the reader's mind and heart, his
work is succinct yet encompassing, accessible yet groundbreaking,
and organically timely. While opening human perception to
spirituality, wonder, desire, love, ethics, and more, Sheldrake's
comprehensive vision brings mysticism to life. To *all* of life."

— Steven Chase, is research fellow at Studium, St. Benedict's
    Monastery, editor of the journal *Spiritus*, and author of
    *Nature as Spiritual Practice, Job: A Theological
    Commentary on the Bible*, and *Angelic Spirituality:
    Medieval Perspectives on the Ways of Angels*

A World Transfigured

The Mystical Journey

Philip Sheldrake

LITURGICAL PRESS
ACADEMIC

Collegeville, Minnesota
www.litpress.org

1	2	3	4	5	6	7	8	9

Library of Congress Cataloging-in-Publication Data

Names: Sheldrake, Philip, author.
Title: A world transfigured : the mystical journey / Philip Sheldrake.
Description: Collegeville, Minnesota : Liturgical Press Academic, [2022] | Includes bibliographical references and index. | Summary: "In A World Transfigured: The Mystical Journey, Philip Sheldrake demonstrates the importance of the mystical dimension of religious belief and practice"— Provided by publisher.
Identifiers: LCCN 2022014798 (print) | LCCN 2022014799 (ebook) | ISBN 9780814685129 (paperback) | ISBN 9780814685372 (epub) | ISBN 9780814685372 (pdf)
Subjects: LCSH: Mysticism. | Rahner, Karl, 1904-1984. | Certeau, Michel de. | BISAC: RELIGION / Mysticism
Classification: LCC BV5082.3 .S49 2022 (print) | LCC BV5082.3 (ebook) | DDC 149/.3—dc23/eng/20220606
LC record available at https://lccn.loc.gov/2022014798
LC ebook record available at https://lccn.loc.gov/2022014799

To Susie

CONTENTS

PREFACE

There is a notable decline in institutional religion in Western countries, especially but not exclusively involving Christianity. However, at the same time, there continues to be a fascination with spirituality, including "the mystical."

My book is not intended to be narrowly academic, nor will it exclusively explore Christian mysticism. Rather, I hope that it will reach an intelligent and thoughtful general readership. The main focus of the book is thematic, with the central chapters focusing on what I identify as five different "styles" or "dimensions" of mysticism, illustrated by examples. Overall, the book will look at how the concepts of "mysticism" and "mystics" have been conventionally understood and interpreted. It will then ask what would be a reasonable approach these days. The book will also show how mystical writings in particular religions have sometimes been influenced from outside. For example, some Christians drew upon Jewish mysticism and Sufi mysticism.

In Part One, chapter 1 asks what we mean by the word "mysticism" and outlines several approaches to the question. The chapter also outlines the five "styles" or dimensions of mysticism that form the main part of the book. Chapter 2 then explores briefly how "mysticism" necessarily connects

with beliefs of some kind, whether religious or not. In Part
Two, as already noted, the five chapters will explore different
approaches to mysticism, illustrated by some examples. Finally,
my conclusion will briefly outline the groundbreaking work
of the French Jesuit scholar, the late Michel de Certeau, who
was a major influence in shaping modern understandings of
mysticism. The conclusion will then end with a brief overview
of how I believe mysticism connects with aspects of contemporary experience.

This book follows on naturally from my earlier book published by Liturgical Press, *The Spiritual Way: Classic Traditions
and Contemporary Practice* (2019). Once again, I wish to
thank Hans Christoffersen at Liturgical Press for encouraging
me to write the new book. I am also particularly grateful to
Oblate School of Theology in San Antonio, Texas, where I
am a professor and director of the Institute for the Study of
Contemporary Spirituality. This has given me opportunities
to give public lectures on various aspects of mysticism, to
take part in conferences hosted by the school, and to teach
graduate courses on the mysticism of Julian of Norwich. I
have also written articles in two journals based at the school,
Offerings and *Spiritus*. I also want to thank the ecumenical
Cambridge Theological Federation and the Von Hügel Institute at St Edmund's College, University of Cambridge, for
my research roles.

As always, I dedicate this book to Susie whose partner-
ship, love, and insightful comments have been very helpful
throughout. I am also very grateful for Susie's beautiful and
imaginative cover design for this book.

Philip Sheldrake
San Antonio and Cambridge, 2021

INTRODUCTION

Toward the end of his life, the great German Jesuit theologian Karl Rahner confronted what he saw as the slow decline of institutional Christianity by promoting the vital importance of the mystical dimension of religious belief and practice. Not long before Rahner died in 1984, his famous aphorism asserted unequivocally that Christians in the future will either be mystics or nothing at all. In his own words, "The devout Christian of the future will either be a 'mystic,' one who has experienced 'something,' or he will cease to be anything at all."[1] Basically, Karl Rahner did not view mysticism as limited to a special class of people. He understood everyone as *homo mysticus*—that is, as inherently oriented toward the transcendent. In the context of our contemporary Western world, it seems likely that this judgment by Karl Rahner applies not only to Christians but also to people associated with the other world religions.

In my view, Karl Rahner's standpoint does not imply that the mystic Christian simply retreats from the outer public world into some kind of protected interior private space. As

---

1. Karl Rahner, "Christian Living Formerly and Today," in *Theological Investigations*, vol. 7 (New York: Herder & Herder, 1971), 15.

Rahner knew perfectly well, Christian discipleship is always embedded in human everyday contexts because these are the "place" of the self-revelation of an ultimately mysterious God. As early as the 1970s, Rahner had suggested that the movement of God's Spirit spread throughout the world far more widely than the institutional Church was prepared to admit. For Rahner, God's outward action implicitly "inspires" or "in-Spirits" the world as a whole in ways that drive people onward in a restless movement toward their ultimate fulfilment. This is a dispersed mysticism of everyday life in the world of ordinary spaces. In the words of Karl Rahner,

> If and insofar as the experience of the Spirit I talk of here is also to be found in a mysticism of everyday life outside a verbalized and institutionalized Christianity, and therefore may be discovered by Christians in their lives when they encounter their non-Christian brothers and sisters . . . Christians need not be shocked or astonished at such a revelation. It should serve only to show that their God, the God of Jesus Christ, wants *all* men and women to be saved, and offers God's grace as liberation to *all* human beings, offering it as liberation into incomprehensible mystery. Then the grace of Christ takes effect in a mysterious way beyond the bounds of verbalized and institutionalized Christendom.[2]

Of course, Karl Rahner's language continued to be explicitly Christian. However, his continual refusal to create a definitive systematic theology was implicitly a defense of God's ultimate mystery and of the limitations of theological language when confronting what Karl Rahner perceived to be the essentially mystical heart of Christianity. This approach was expressed

2. Karl Rahner, *The Spirit in the Church*, ET extract in G. Kelly, ed., *Karl Rahner: Theologian of the Graced Search for Meaning* (Minneapolis: Fortress Press, 1992), 233–34.

more and more strongly as Rahner grew older, not least in some of his ideas that were only published posthumously:

> The true system of thought really is the knowledge that humanity is finally directed precisely not toward what it can control in knowledge but toward the absolute mystery as such; that mystery is . . . the blessed goal of knowledge which comes to itself when it is with the incomprehensible one. . . . In other words, then, the system is the system of what cannot be systematized.[3]

In his final meditations on God and essays on spirituality, Rahner affirmed the ultimate unknowability of God in ways that were much more explicit and robust than in his earlier writings. It is not too far-fetched to suggest that as he became older, Karl Rahner became increasingly skeptical about the dogmatic pretensions of the institutional Church as well as about conventional approaches to theological certainties.

The main focus of this book on mysticism is thematic, with the five chapters of Part Two focusing on what I identify as five different, but nonexclusive, approaches to mysticism, illustrated by examples taken mainly from Christianity but also with some from other religions. Overall, the book will look at how the concepts of "mysticism" and "mystics" have conventionally been understood and interpreted. The book will also show how mystical writings in a particular religious tradition such as Christianity have sometimes been influenced from outside the tradition. For example, some Christian mystics drew upon Jewish mysticism and Sufi mysticism.

In chapter 1, "What is Mysticism?" I ask what exactly the concepts of "mysticism" and "mystics" mean, why mysticism fascinates so many people in Western countries these days, and why mysticism is important from a wider human standpoint, as

---

3. In P. Imhof and H. Biallowons, ed., *Karl Rahner in Dialogue* (New York: Crossroad, 1986), 196–97.

well as from a specifically religious one. The chapter briefly outlines some influential theories and interpretations of mysticism and examines the current state of the question. I then offer my own summary definition. The chapter also asks whether mystics are a special category of people or whether "the mystical" actually touches the lives of a much wider range of people.

In chapter 2, "Mysticism and Beliefs," I explore whether we can actually separate mysticism from our systems of belief. In his *The Varieties of Religious Experience*, the still-influential late nineteenth-century psychologist and philosopher William James focused on a universalist understanding of mysticism related to interior experience. William James asserted that such interior spiritual experience was essentially a "pure consciousness event" that crossed the boundaries between different religions and transcended belief systems. Nowadays, his assumptions are seriously questioned. In contrast to James, I believe that we can never effectively separate experience from our frameworks of meaning and beliefs. So the chapter goes on to explore briefly how mysticism necessarily connects with beliefs of some kind, whether these are religious or not.

In Part Two, as I have already noted, the main chapters will explore the five different approaches to mysticism that I identify, illustrated by examples. These are: "Love and Desire"; "Knowing and Unknowing"; "Beauty"; "Mysticism and Everyday Practice"; and finally, "The Mystic as Radical Prophet."

Finally, my conclusion will outline how the groundbreaking work on mysticism by the multidisciplinary French Jesuit scholar, Michel de Certeau, has been a major influence in shaping modern approaches to mysticism. In particular, de Certeau underlines that mysticism draws us beyond the tangible and the definable. Certeau's method emphasizes that religion, especially spirituality, involves an endless journey beyond fixed points in our quest for a God who is ultimately unnameable, indefinable, and uncontrollable.

part
one

The Concept
of Mysticism

CHAPTER ONE

WHAT IS MYSTICISM?

This opening chapter explores what exactly the concept of "mysticism" means. Why does mysticism fascinate so many people these days? Is the notion of "mysticism"—and its reality—important in relation to wider human existence, as well as to a specifically religious life? First of all, I will briefly outline some influential theories and interpretations of mysticism. I will also examine the current state of the question of how people understand mysticism. Having offered my own brief summary definition of mysticism, this opening chapter goes on to ask whether people known as "mystics" are a special category or whether in some sense "the mystical" touches the lives of a wide range of people. This raises the question of whether mysticism is necessarily explicitly religious. Is it essentially associated with intense spiritual practices and, if so, is this open to everyone or only to a select few? Is mysticism essentially experiential? Does it involve only trancelike states or ecstatic experiences—for example, visions? Or does mysticism suggest more broadly a transfiguration of how people experience or understand the everyday world? How does mysticism relate to our ways of "knowing" in relation to the transcendent, whether this is understood as a personal God or not?

This introductory chapter will also briefly mention interesting examples of crossovers between different religions—for example, the historic connections between Jewish mysticism or Sufi mysticism and writings and people within the Christian tradition.

Finally, the chapter will outline the five different approaches to mysticism that form the main chapters of the book, that is: "Love and Desire"; "Knowing and Unknowing"; "Beauty"; "Mysticism and Everyday Practice"; and finally, "The Mystic as Radical Prophet."

REASONS FOR CURRENT INTEREST

Judging by the religion or mind/body/spirit sections of large bookstores in the United Kingdom and the United States, there is a peculiar fascination with mysticism these days. Not so long ago, I was in a Barnes & Noble bookstore where there was a section entitled "Supernatural & Mystical," in which the books were basically about astrology and tarot! The word "mysticism" seems to be often used nowadays to refer to anything esoteric, particularly if it promises special insight, wisdom, or the key to life. The notion of "mysticism" generally implies that one can have an immediate encounter with and perhaps immediate knowledge of the mystery of God. In other words, mysticism seems to imply some kind of direct and personal *experience*, in contrast to the way people usually think about religion—that is, structures, rituals, doctrines, morals, and laws. Indeed, mysticism is, like the associated word "spirituality," sometimes contrasted favorably with "religion" in this structural sense. Sometimes mysticism is seen as the essence of all true religion behind the different religious languages we use about God, implying a common stream running through all the great religions, from Roman Catholicism to Tibetan Buddhism—but in a way that is not ultimately dependent on their differences.

In my estimation, the reality is less dramatic. Yet why is there such a fascination with mysticism these days? I detect two main and closely related reasons. Both have to do with what I would call the crises of our modern world and consequently also with an intense emotional need. First of all, many people desire to transcend limitations and boundaries and to experience a sense of union with other people or with the natural world around them. People want to overcome the profound divisions within humanity, whether these are political, religious, or cultural, because they experience them as deeply painful and destructive. As a result, many people look for something "in common" on a spiritual level. However, because the first port of call, organized religion, appears to be riven with mutual suspicion, people increasingly look for spiritual contexts that bypass these deeply unattractive realities.

Second, a variety of contemporary social, economic, and political factors make many people suspicious about the capacity of a purely material existence and enhancement to fulfill their deepest human aspirations. Thus, the existential crisis of meaning, fears for the future of humanity, a certain cynicism about humanly created structures (politics or the church), may be overcome by appealing to a level of consciousness that is available intuitively rather than by more intellectual, rational, and moralizing means. "Mysticism" therefore seems to offer an essentially noncognitive connection with the very depths of human existence.

As I have already noted, the notion of mysticism, alongside the concept of spirituality, provokes a great deal of fascination in our contemporary Western culture. Unfortunately, people often assume that the word mysticism basically refers to something esoteric or deeply mysterious, particularly if it seems to promise us some kind of special insight or deep experience of a sense of connectedness to nature or to the greater cosmos. In some people's minds, mysticism is also frequently associated with strange experiences such as trancelike states or visions. In terms of the world religions, mysticism is present in some form in all of them and is given a special status. How does mysticism relate to the concept of spirituality? These days, the two words are sometimes treated as if they are basically the same. However, if we study the spiritual traditions of the various world faiths, we will see that spirituality is the broader term because it embraces a committed approach to human existence, for example as "the Christian life" or "the Jewish life." "The mystical" is simply one dimension of this broader religious life or one manifestation of it.

A Problem of Definition

Scholars and writers on the subject of spirituality often note that both terms, "spirituality" and "mysticism," are equally difficult to define in a straightforward way.[1] In terms of the various world religions, ideas such as direct access to the transcendent or an immediate personal contact with God are fairly common. Beyond the boundaries of religion and irrespective of religious beliefs, more broadly based transcendent experiences are recorded by quite a number of people. Trancelike states may sometimes be artificially induced by drugs. However, the kind of oceanic experiences of connection with nature and a transfiguration or illumination of surroundings are generally not artificially induced but happen spontaneously and are often totally unexpected. I am personally aware of people who have had such dramatic moments of illumination. Among the most common contexts for such experiences is the sense of overwhelming awe in the face of nature—for example, mystical experiences can be provoked by the power of the ocean or the majesty of mountains. Another medium for mystical experiences is aesthetic, particularly a sense of being overwhelmed emotionally or lifted up to "another place" while listening to music.

1. E.g., see Paul Oliver, *Mysticism: A Guide for the Perplexed* (London: Bloomsbury, 2009), especially chapter 1, "The Concept of Mysticism."

It seems that the actual term "mysticism" first appeared in France (as "*la mystique*") in the seventeenth century.[2] Thus, rather like the concept of "spirituality," the word "mysticism" began its life in a Christian context, even though it has since been adopted by other religions and also beyond the boundaries of religion. To some observers, both then and now, the word "mysticism" seems to point to a separate, somewhat eccentric side of religion or of spiritual experience. For some people, the word simply implies that "weird things happen to strange people." Some other observers, particularly those involved in the institutional side of religion, view the idea of "mysticism" and of people called "mystics" with profound suspicion. For example, in the words of the nineteenth-century English Benedictine monk and historian, Cardinal Gasquet, mysticism "begins in mist and ends in schism." For such people, "mysticism" contrasts dangerously with the institutional side of religion, such as authority structures, systems of doctrine, religious laws, and formal rituals. Indeed, mysticism is often treated with suspicion by religious authorities because it appears to promote a form of direct inspiration by God that bypasses religious authority and an orthodox religious path. Hence Cardinal Gasquet's references to "mist," that is, a lack of doctrinal precision, and "schism," that is, the danger of rejecting religious authority and established religious systems.

Until relatively recently, most commentators have focused on mysticism simply as a category of religious *experience*. This approach results in a number of problems. First, it tends to separate mysticism from the core beliefs of any particular religion and intellectual reflection upon these (what Christians refer to as theology). In other words, mysticism becomes distinct from the ways we try to think about or speak about God or ultimate reality. Second, such a narrowly experiential

2. On the history of the word, see Michel de Certeau, *The Mystic Fable* (Chicago: University of Chicago Press, 1992).

approach removes mysticism from the public world into a private realm of personal interiority. One result is that it becomes difficult to see how mysticism may be of any great importance to the vast majority of people—whether within a particular religion or in wider society. Third, and related to this inwardness, such an experiential approach tends to concentrate on mystical phenomena or "states of mind" and emotions experienced by a very limited number of people as the result of their intense meditative practice or their ascetical discipline.

Given that a mystical dimension is said to exist in all world religions, all of these approaches raise the question about whether there may be a "something" which we can call "mysticism as such" that transcends the boundaries of particular religious and spiritual traditions. This seems to be a common viewpoint in many modern popular writings and workshops on mysticism, especially those influenced by so-called New Age spirituality, with its innate suspicion of old-fashioned and closed dogmatic systems.

Universal Mysticism?

The notion of "mysticism as such," or universal mysticism, which we can think of as set apart from specific religious belief systems, is broadly the viewpoint of the still-influential writings of the American philosopher and psychologist of religion, William James, in his Gifford Lectures, *The Varieties of Religious Experience*, which first appeared in 1902. His emphasis was on interior religion rather than on its external forms.[3] For James, what he thought of as interior religion was to be understood as a global, universal phenomenon. He interpreted religious experience, including the mystical, as a "pure consciousness event" that exists prior to any form of religious definition or

---

3. William James, *The Varieties of Religious Experience* (New York: Classic Books International, 2010).

any specific belief system. However, there are a number of problems with this approach.

First, any attempt at an all-inclusive definition of mysticism is open to the criticism that it fails to do justice to the riches and complexities of specific religious traditions, such as Christianity, Islam, or Buddhism. Such all-inclusive definitions are highly abstract and are not what the people we call "mystics" say about their understanding of the spiritual path. The point is that any adequate theory of mysticism must not begin with some abstract "essence" of mysticism but with an awareness of specific personalities, historical moments, and cultural-religious contexts. Indeed, the people we refer to as "mystics" did not set out to practice something called "mysticism." On the contrary, religious mystics are people who seek to practice their specific religious faith with particular commitment and intensity. In terms of the theistic religions, mysticism involves an explicit awareness of the immediate presence of God. Throughout history, the great mystical writers are clear that what they are concerned about is fundamentally a spiritual way of life, including service to other people, rather than having intense inner experiences or achieving altered states of consciousness.

Second, in the strongly scriptural and text-based Abrahamic religions, Judaism, Christianity, and Islam, the mystical tradition is as concerned with religious language as it is with spiritual experiences. It can be understood as the quest to reach out to a God who is ultimately beyond our capacity to capture in definitions. In other words, the mystical traditions of these religions effectively question the adequacy of all the words we seek to use about God and about the transcendent. Can we ultimately define or name God? The mystical traditions of Judaism, Christianity, and Islam are clear that the answer is no. As the great medieval German Christian mystic, Meister Eckhart, said of God in one of his sermons, "If I have spoken of it [the divine], I have not spoken, for it is ineffable."

Modern philosophical treatments of mysticism, such as those promoted by Steven Katz, also call into question the notion that mystical experience is fundamentally the same in all religions and that mystics of different faiths merely describe their experiences and illuminations after the event in the religious language and imagery that is familiar to them. The implication of these philosophical critiques of William James's notion of a common "mystical core" in all religions is that it is not really possible to distinguish our experience from our interpretations of it. In fact, we can only experience things within our established frameworks of meaning. Thus, what we refer to as Christian mysticism is particular, as is Jewish mysticism or Buddhist mysticism. The focus of any religious mysticism is quite specific because the people we call mystics experience in the way they do within, rather than despite, their framework of beliefs. In other words, the experiences of mystics are preformed by their background assumptions, which set the boundaries within which any actual experience takes place. Indeed, the moment we name something as a "religious" experience, specifically an experience of God, we have already interpreted it.[4]

If we reject the idea that there is a definable, common "something" that we can call "mysticism as such," that exists prior to and independently of specific religious traditions, can we talk meaningfully at all about a mystical dimension present in all world religions? For example, by using the word "mysticism" in reference to Buddhism or Islam, are we not simply borrowing a concept from Christianity and then imposing it on other religions? However, in order to validate the use of the word "mysticism" so broadly, we are not bound to fall back on the work of William James and his belief that there is a shared "something" that predates religious belief systems. However, it would be fair to say that, as with the word "spirituality," it is possible to detect some "family resemblances"

---

4. See, e.g., Steven Katz, ed., *Mysticism and Philosophical Analysis* (Oxford: Oxford University Press, 1978), and Steven Katz, ed., *Mysticism and Language* (Oxford: Oxford University Press, 1992).

that enable us to explore a similar concern with mysticism within all the world religions. This relates to a spiritual life that is intensely penetrated by the presence of God or, more broadly, the Transcendent.

For me, mysticism is an intensification of the spiritual path within Christianity and the other world religions. In Christian terms, this involves a deepened consciousness of God's transforming presence within us and around us that seeks to lead us onwards to seek a mysterious "beyond" or an "always more." In the early Church, that is, the so-called patristic period, the very heart of Christian theology was mystical. Theology reflected on how every baptized Christian was drawn into the divine mystery through belonging to the "fellowship of the mystery," that is, the Christian community. Here, believers were exposed to God through the Scriptures and also via participation in the liturgy—the "sacred mysteries." In this way, every Christian is potentially a "mystic" in the sense that their Christian lives plunge all of them into the mystery of God-in-Christ.[5]

However, this deepened consciousness also calls into question our limited language about the nature of God and leads us beyond conventional religious definitions to touch ultimate and indefinable mystery. In this sense, mysticism, like spirituality more broadly, concerns the whole process of life rather than merely being a question of dramatically altered states of consciousness. Everyday life experience is transformed into something wondrous. "Mystical moments" or a life lived persistently "on the edge" relates to our overall presence and action in the world. In that sense, "the mystical" is necessarily linked to ethical action and to a quest for social as well as personal transformation.

---

5. See Louis Bouyer, "Mysticism: An Essay on the History of the Word," in *Understanding Mysticism*, ed. Richard Woods (London: Athlone Press, 1980); also, Andrew Louth, *The Origins of the Christian Mystical Tradition* (Oxford: Oxford University Press, 1981).

MYSTICISM AND MIXTURES

Any careful historical study of a specific religion—or of religion in general—soon reveals that no religious system of belief and practice is utterly pure. Indeed, mystics from different religious traditions, particularly the Abrahamic religions, Judaism, Christianity, and Islam, have actually consciously borrowed from each other's traditions across time.

To take simply one example, even though Christianity is profoundly concerned with its belief in the uniqueness of God's self-revelation in the person of Jesus and was subsequently preoccupied with precise doctrinal definitions, it was also receptive to influences from beyond its boundaries from the very start. Of course, its overall origins were as a particular group within Judaism that then slowly parted company with the synagogue. Almost as soon as Christianity began to spread throughout the cities of the Roman Empire, it encountered ancient philosophical traditions which it was able to detach from their pre-Christian Greek or Roman frameworks and then draw upon. One particular school of philosophy, Greek Neoplatonism, had an early impact on what we might call the mystical interpretation of the Christian spiritual path. For example, the third-century theologian Origen in the city of Alexandria drew inspiration from the Neoplatonic emphasis on a spiritual path leading to union with "the One" or God. This union was attained through contemplation and mystical interpretations of the Scriptures, as well as through an ethical life that was purified from whatever diluted our desire for union with the One. Such Neoplatonic thinking was also adopted by later Christian mystical theologians, such as the Egyptian monk Evagrius in the fourth century. Evagrius described God mainly in terms of "negative" language—that is, he emphasized what God is not. He also taught a related form of imageless contemplative prayer. Later, at the beginning of the fifth century, an anonymous monk from Syria, known as pseudo-Dionysius, was also influenced by ancient Greek philosophy. Among his highly influential works was his *Mystical Theology*, which stresses the theme of divine darkness. That is, the reality of God is ultimately beyond all names and definitions. This work, along with the other writings by pseudo-Dionysius, had a major impact on the development of Western Christian mysticism during the Middle Ages.

Later, during the European Middle Ages, there was a notable interchange, particularly in Spain, between Christian mysticism and the other two Abrahamic religions. One notable example is the thirteenth-century Catalan philosopher, poet, and mystic Ramon Llull. It is now accepted that Llull learned Arabic primarily in order to dialogue with Islamic thought rather than to convert Muslims to Christianity. In his famous mystical work, *The Book of the Lover and Beloved*, Ramon Llull was inspired by Sufi Islam, not least by the great Muslim thinker Al-Ghazzali. It also seems that important themes in the particular version of Sufism present in Al-Andalus had an impact on sixteenth-century Franciscan mystical writers such as Francisco de Osuna, who in turn influenced the great Carmelite mystical writer Teresa of Avila. More controversially, some scholars believe that Sufism also had an impact on the language and symbolism in the poetry of the other great Spanish Carmelite mystic, John of the Cross, as well as on his mystical treatise the *Spiritual Canticle*. An example is the image of ecstatic fire and burning flames of love in John of the Cross's poem *Llama de amor viva* (*The Living Flame of Love*), as well as the imagery of flowing water and of the fountain of the soul in his spiritual treatise, the *Spiritual Canticle*. It is also worth noting that it is now widely accepted that both Teresa of Avila and John of the Cross had Jewish ancestry and, in particular, that the Jewish mystical text *Zohar* may have influenced Teresa's great mystical work *The Interior Castle*.

At an earlier stage, Sufism also influenced Judaism. An interesting example was Abraham Maimuni, the son of the twelfth-century Spanish Jewish philosopher Maimonides, who had died in Egypt. Maimuni is credited with bringing the Sufi practice known as *dhikr*, the meditative recitation of God's names, into Jewish spiritual practice. Maimuni's followers in Egypt created a Jewish Sufi movement associated with spiritual guides who practiced spiritual retreats and undertook ascetical practices such as solitude and fasting. This movement survived into the fifteenth century.

The notion of any reciprocal influence by Christianity on Islam is more controversial. However, some scholars believe that at an early stage of its existence, the Sufi mystical tradition's practice of meditation involving controlled breathing was influenced by the Eastern Christian monastic tradition. This is the practice of still contemplative prayer that became known as Hesychasm (from the Greek word *hesychia* or stillness).

MYSTICISM AND VISIONS

Some mystical writings, for example in Christianity, refer to visionary experiences. As I have already indicated, I do not wish to limit our understanding of mysticism to intense inner experiences in isolation. However, there is no doubt that some people have these kinds of experiences, which are commonly referred to as mystical. Such experiences may indicate a person having reached a deep level of union with God or with a more undefined ultimate transcendent reality. However, the notion of union with God (or an immediacy of presence to the divine) is far more important than particular kinds of experience. In reality, not all the people we call mystics have experienced what we might call ecstatic experiences or visions or other altered states of consciousness. We also need to be careful because, on their own, such extraordinary experiences are not reliable indicators of the mystical. For example, it is possible that a visionary experience may result from a psychotic episode. Equally, as already noted, ecstasy—a trancelike state in which a person transcends normal consciousness—may be achieved artificially by deliberately taking drugs or by sleep deprivation or by fasting.

I have already suggested that religious mysticism is closely related to living out the spiritual path within a particular religion. Equally, because for religious people what we call God is a reality ultimately beyond our ability to control or define, many mystics insist that a true consciousness of the divine is best realized through an experience of absence, of darkness, or of a "cloud of unknowing" (to borrow from the famous fourteenth-century English mystical text of the same name). That is, through a process of negation or denial, all experiences, images, or definitions of the divine are ultimately stripped away. In this way, the person on a spiritual journey moves towards the ultimate mystery of God or the transcendent that lies beyond both definitions and denial.

Some modern scholars of Christian mysticism, such as Bernard McGinn, have also questioned whether visions are truly mystical. This suspicion led McGinn in his magisterial history of Christian mysticism to leave out of consideration some well-known medieval women candidates for the title of mystic. One example is the highly popular figure of Hildegard of Bingen, who also wrote extraordinary music and poetry and created artwork.[6] While, as I have suggested, visionary experiences alone, or indeed a whole array of paranormal phenomena, do not necessarily imply mystical experience, there is an equal danger in rejecting them entirely. In a certain context, intense experiences such as visions or ecstasy may be a preparation for a heightened awareness of the transforming presence of the divine. In other words, such phenomena are sometimes authentic indicators of spiritual transformation.

6. Bernard McGinn's ongoing series is entitled *The Presence of God: A History of Western Christian Mysticism* (New York: Crossroad, 1991–). Six volumes have been published as of Spring 2021 (vol. VI has three parts).

Other Christian scholars of mysticism, such as the feminist thinker, the late Grace Jantzen, have pointed out that visionary experiences were also a source of authority, as well as a validation of spiritual teaching, for certain groups of people (for example, women during the Middle Ages) who otherwise lacked official status or authority in the Christian church.[7] Thus, in the fourteenth century, it is significant that the immensely popular English mystical writer, Julian of Norwich, begins her writing with the sixteen visions (or "showings") that she experienced while seriously ill. These were not presented as ends in themselves but as the basis for introducing her sophisticated theological reflections and spiritual teachings.[8] Indeed, great mystical writers such as Julian are not interested in visionary experience as such nor in the status it gives them. What concerns them is what such privileged experiences reveal and enable them to teach for the benefit of others. While visions and other paranormal phenomena are by definition extraordinary, to exclude the "extraordinary" automatically from our considerations runs the risk of setting aside anything that seems peculiar or that makes us uncomfortable because it does not fit with our contemporary cultural assumptions.

MYSTICISM AND UNION

One word that is frequently used by both mystics and by commentators on mysticism to describe the heart of mystical

7. Grace Jantzen, *Power, Gender, and Christian Mysticism* (Cambridge: Cambridge University Press, 1995).

8. For accessible editions of Julian's writings in modern English, see Elizabeth Spearing, ed., *Julian of Norwich: Revelations of Divine Love* (London: Penguin Classics, 1998); Edmund Colledge and James Walsh, ed., *Julian of Norwich: Showings*, Classics of Western Spirituality (Mahwah, NJ: Paulist Press, 1978); and, more recently, Barry Windeatt, ed., *Julian of Norwich: Revelations of Divine Love*, Oxford World Classics (Oxford: Oxford University Press, 2015).

experience is "union" with God or with the Absolute. That is, the mystical path involves the pursuit of union with God or with whatever one defines as ultimate reality. For example, there are versions of mysticism in Christianity that speak of "union" but maintain a clear distinction between "the human self" and God. Other mystical traditions suggest that "the self," in the sense of freestanding individuality, is extinguished and finally left behind. Examples include the concept of *fana* in Islamic Sufism or that everything is absorbed into the One or into absolute reality as in Taoism or the concept of *maha-mudra* in Northern Buddhism. The monotheistic Abrahamic religions of Judaism, Christianity, and Islam are in general terms particularly sensitive to the need to maintain the absolute sovereignty, independence, and "otherness" of God. They are thus suspicious of any dangerous language of human identity with, let alone mystical absorption into, the divine. However, to be fair, in the mysticism of all three Abrahamic religions there is a degree of ambiguity in the language that is used. Certainly, the concept of human surrender to God, the sacrifice of the self or loss of the human ego and intimate communion with God, is powerfully present in different forms.

Is "union" with God or the Absolute the end of the matter? Interestingly, in certain approaches to the mystical in Christian tradition, the deep union with God expressed by such people as Bernard of Clairvaux, Francis of Assisi, Catherine of Siena, or Jan Ruusbroec led them into greater activity and service of others, rather than into the opposite. We shall briefly explore the connections between mysticism and social transformation in chapter 7.

A broad and flexible understanding of mysticism need not take the language of union with God as the defining characteristic. While many mystics have used such language, others have avoided it and preferred different ways of expressing things. A broad understanding of mysticism also emphasizes that it is essentially a commitment of our lives directed at reaching the divine. The significance of the effect of mystical consciousness on the life of the mystic is important because religious traditions have in some sense always implied that the only way to validate the claims of mystics is through the impact that their inner transformation has upon their lives and their relationships with other people. Seeing mysticism as part of a life process rather than merely as a set of experiences also emphasizes that it is an element within a religious tradition rather than some kind of esoteric alternative to conventional religion.

IMAGES AND IMAGELESSNESS

For example, in Christian approaches to mysticism, the classic teaching is that on the spiritual journey there is a movement ever onward towards greater simplicity and stillness, as well as a growing realization of the inadequacy of all human images of the divine and language about God. However, a common approach in early Christianity usually involved some version of a simple, twofold path.

The first path is sometimes known as the "apophatic" way, from the Greek word *apophasis* or denial. This way of "denial" or "unknowing" is associated with imagelessness, stillness, and wordlessness in our engagement with God. Rather than attempt to describe what God or the Absolute "is," the apophatic way suggests that we simply cannot finally capture God in words or in images. God is beyond all images and all concepts. Thus, everything we seek to affirm about God or the Absolute must in the end be denied or negated as "not God." Examples of this approach are the highly enigmatic writings of the fourteenth-century mystical writers Meister Eckhart in Germany or the anonymous author of *The Cloud of Unknowing* in England. Similar trends can be found in other religions. For example, in Hinduism, Brahman (the supreme soul or the divine) is described in the text of the Upanishads as "neither this, not that." In classic Buddhism, this apophatic approach is apparent in much of its literature. According to early texts, the Buddha refused to answer certain questions about ultimate reality, such as the existence of the human soul, the origin of the cosmos, and life beyond death. Some commentators also suggest that the Buddha had an apophatic approach to the question of the existence or otherwise of a God or gods. All that he would say is that we do not need a God to save us. In that sense, Buddhism is more accurately described as nontheistic rather than as atheistic.

The second path in mysticism is known in Christianity as the "kataphatic way." This involves our attempts to speak of the divine through positive language or images. In Christianity this "way" may embrace a devotional focus, for example on the person of Jesus Christ (as in the writings of Francis of Assisi) or the use of imagination or images in prayer and meditation (for example, in the *Spiritual Exercises* of Ignatius Loyola). As an example in other religions, the school of Vaishnavism in Hinduism uses positive theological language about the qualities of the Supreme Lord Krishna or Vishnu.

In fact, in the Christian mystical tradition there is no basis for any *absolute* distinction between the apophatic (negative) and kataphatic (positive) "ways." The logic of Christian understandings of the divine is that God is both revealed in and through the Scriptures, our images, everyday experiences, relationships, and the world around us and yet, at the same time, is always more than these. Really, the negative and positive "ways" are not alternative types of mysticism but are two dimensions of all mysticism. In differing ways, there is a balance between the use of images for God or the Absolute and a necessary imagelessness in all mystical traditions. Both approaches reveal something of God yet, by definition, neither is capable of finally capturing the fullness of the divine.

I have already suggested that I do not believe in some kind of universal mysticism but understand it to be distinctive in relation to each religion, even if the notion of "mysticism" has some shared characteristics. In the next chapter, "Mysticism and Beliefs," I will explore the ways in which mysticism connects with beliefs—mainly in relation to Christianity and its theology but with some references to other religions and also to esoteric movements.

The Dimensions of Mysticism

In Part Two of this book, I will outline my five approaches to mysticism. The first approach, "Love and Desire," explores how the theme of love, desire, and longing is a powerful one in the mystical writings of Christianity and beyond. Some mystics emphasized the ecstatic nature of love and desire. Our longing and desire reflect God's powerful longing within us and leads us to an intimate encounter with God. The book in the Jewish Scriptures known as the Song of Songs is a collection of powerful love poems spoken alternately by a woman and a man. In both Jewish and later Christian writers, this was interpreted allegorically as expressing the passion of divine-human love. The book had an extensive influence on Christian mystical writings. The themes of love and desire also appear in what is known as the "bridal mysticism" of such medieval women writers as the Beguines (for example, Hadewijch) in Germany and the Low Countries and in the English woman writer, Julian of Norwich. Later, love and desire were powerfully present in the sixteenth-century Spanish Carmelite mystical writers, Teresa of Avila and John of the Cross, and also in the seventeenth-century Anglican poet, priest, theologian, and spiritual writer Thomas Traherne. Beyond Christian mysticism, love and desire is also a powerful theme in the two major Jewish mystical traditions of Kabbalah and Hasidism. The theme appears in Islam, notably in Sufi mysticism—for example, in the poetry of Rumi and also in Al-Ghazzali. Finally, and more controversially, the motif of desire appears in the work of twentieth-century Dutch writer Etty Hillesum, who was from a secular Jewish family and died in Auschwitz. Over time, Hillesum entered into an unconventional but deep spiritual journey expressed in her diaries and her letters. Her restless longing, desire, and intense spiritual passion, although detached from institutional religion, gave a profoundly mystical tone to her writings and led her to an encounter with what she called "the God within."

The second mystical approach, "Knowing and Unknowing," explores the themes of "illumination" or "knowing" as another striking aspect of mystical writings. In one sense, mysticism involves a kind of transfiguration of our human ways of knowing and leads to a new level of enlightenment regarding God or the Transcendent. A striking example is the Eastern Orthodox Christian tradition known as Hesychasm. Its medieval version (for example, in Gregory Palamas) outlines a way of knowing that transcends thoughts and images. The famous practice popularly known as the Jesus Prayer underpins an inner spiritual awareness of the presence of the Spirit of God that may evoke a luminous vision of the transcendent. However, in relation to an ultimately mysterious God (or the Absolute), there is necessarily a permanent tension between knowing and unknowing in relation to our human capacity to touch the divine. To what extent can we be said to have knowledge of God or of the Absolute? Or, in the words of the anonymous fourteenth-century English mystical text, *The Cloud of Unknowing*, "How am I to think of God and what is he? And to this I can only answer 'I do not know.'" There is also the enigmatic theological language of the popular Rhineland mystic Meister Eckhart, who talked about the need for us to deny the ways we seek to define God in order to touch the divine "ground." This is what we may think of as "the God beyond God." Eckhart also loved to say that "If I have spoken of it [God], I have not spoken, for it [God] is ineffable." Within Islam, the Sufism of Al-Ghazali also touched upon the theme of a deeper "knowing" in relation to Allah and to the

Koran. The Jewish Kabbalah text, *The Zohar* (which, as I have already noted, may have influenced the Christian mystic Teresa of Avila), discussed reaching a deeper mystical knowledge of the Torah; that is, the law of God as revealed in the books of the Pentateuch. Finally, a quest for hidden knowledge of reality or for superior illumination is also a characteristic of what are known as "esoteric movements," such as Theosophy (which influenced the mystic theory of the Russian composer Alexander Scriabin) or Anthroposophy (which influenced the spiritual vision of the artist Wassily Kandinsky).

I refer to a third approach to mysticism as "Beauty." In broad terms, there is an intense relationship between a deepened sense of beauty and mystical experience or illumination. This is especially noticeable in the worlds of music, art, and poetic literature. For example, the Russian pianist and composer Alexander Scriabin (who I have just mentioned) developed a kind of mystical theory based on the role of music as the vehicle of a transformation of human perception. Music may sometimes evoke a sense of "oceanic connection" to the Transcendent. Some composers, such as Olivier Messiaen, saw musical sound in itself as spiritual because, in his view, it relates to the universal harmonies of the cosmos. It was said that Messiaen always had his gaze focused on "The Beyond." Other composers with a quasi-mystical sense include John Tavener, a convert to Orthodox Christianity; John Cage, who was influenced by both Zen Buddhism and the Christian mystic Meister Eckhart; and Arvö Part, who is inspired by both Gregorian chant and Eastern Orthodox music. The mystical sense of the painter Wassily Kandinsky has already been mentioned and to him may be added other artists, such as El Greco and Piet Mondrian. The music and widely known poetry of the Sufi writer Rumi is notable, as is the prose poetry of Kahlil Gibran in his extremely popular classic, *The Prophet*. Gibran was a Maronite Christian who was also influenced by the mysticism of Sufi Islam. Other striking examples of poetry with a mystical dimension are the seventeenth-century Anglican George Herbert, one of the greatest English poets, and mystical references in the twentieth-century Welsh poet and Anglican priest, R. S. Thomas. Finally, there is the notion of "nature mysticism," in which engaging with natural elements, such as the ocean, mountains, or wilderness, evokes a sense of liminality—that is, of existing on a boundary between the immediate material world and the transcendent. Examples would be Francis of Assisi's hymn to creation, Thomas Traherne once again, Annie Dillard (*Pilgrim at Tinker Creek*), and Walt Whitman.

My fourth approach to mysticism is what I call "Mysticism and Everyday Practice." A notable example of this—or a "mysticism of the present moment"—is the spirituality of the sixteenth-century writer Ignatius Loyola, expressed particularly in his *Spiritual Exercises* with its powerful theme of "finding God in all things." Another sixteenth-century Spanish mystic, Teresa of Avila, while a monastic nun, was also a down-to-earth person with a strong sense of the spiritual quality of daily work and of charity to other people. A striking twentieth-century example of a mysticism of everyday practice is the book *Markings* by the deeply spiritual secretary general of the United Nations, Dag Hammarskjöld.

Beyond Christianity, the fundamental basis of Jewish mysticism is the practice of a religious life in the everyday world. However, at the heart of Jewish life was also communication with and interaction with a personal God. In the best-known form of Jewish mysticism, the Kabbalah, the quest is for a deeper realization of the Law or Torah. Here, there is an intimate connection between the common Jewish rituals, ethical action, and mystical experience. Turning to Islam, Sufism is perhaps best known for the mystical dimensions of love, knowing, and beauty. However, there is also an emphasis on everyday practice. Sufism suggests that the Qur'an has complex spiritual meanings which may only be appreciated through intense spiritual practice as one leads an everyday life. Finally, I note aspects of the Eastern spiritualities of Hinduism and Buddhism.

I have called the fifth and final approach to mysticism "The Mystic as Radical Prophet." This notion of mystics as expressions of radical spirituality relates to a connection in some mystics between their spiritual journey and ethics, especially a commitment to the promotion of social transformation. The medieval Flemish mystical writer Jan van Ruusbroec believed in an essential connection between contemplation, ethics, and charity. In twentieth-century Christianity, a striking example of this dimension of mysticism is the German pastor and theologian, Dietrich Bonhoeffer, who is described as a mystic in the writings of the theologian Jürgen Moltmann. Bonhoeffer was murdered by the Nazis. Later, the African American theologian Howard Thurman is sometimes described as a mystic because of his intense awareness of the unity of all people and of all reality. Thurman was a major influence on Martin Luther King Jr. and on the American Civil Rights Movement. The theologian and political activist, Dorothee Sölle, was deeply inspired by Christian mysticism and believed that mystical consciousness and the mystical path were the sources both of spiritual healing and of true social resistance. A similar connection between contemplation and social liberation appears in the writings of the liberation theologians Segundo Galilea and Gustavo Gutiérrez.

Finally, within Hinduism, the nineteenth-century guru and mystic Ramakrishna and his pupil Swami Vivekananda both sought in their own ways not only to break down the barriers between "the spiritual" and everyday life but, more radically, to teach that serving the poor and the despised was to serve God. In addition, Swami Vivekananda actively contested British imperialism in India and fought the social injustice of both material poverty and of the Hindu caste system. I end by focusing on Buddhism, especially the contemporary movement called Engaged Buddhism. This is especially associated with the Vietnamese Buddhist monk and writer Thich Nhat Hanh, whose popular writings suggest that responding to human suffering is a critical dimension of deep spiritual practice.

CONCLUSION

Clearly the concept of mysticism is complex—not only because it has significant variations across the different religious traditions but also because it is ambiguous in its overall focus. This applies even in a religious tradition such as Christianity, where the word and concept of mysticism has its origins. By way of summary, what can safely be said is that to limit the notion of mysticism or the mystical path to individual and intense interior experiences is far too narrow. As I have indicated, mysticism is also bound up with questions of language and the use of imagery in reference to God or to a more undefined Absolute. To what degree is it valid to attempt to speak of "God"? As a matter of principle, how important is it that any attempts to name or define the divine are balanced with denial, negation, and imagelessness? Finally, how essential is it to relate the mystical path to the wider question of our presence and action in the everyday world? In other words, as a number of important mystical figures suggest, the notion of mysticism is linked to ethical action and to social transformation. Equally, in the minds of some contemporary writers, "the mystical" is a vital component in any effective quest for social justice.

CHAPTER TWO

MYSTICISM AND BELIEFS

C an we separate mysticism from our beliefs? As I mentioned in the previous chapter, the still-influential late nineteenth-century psychologist and philosopher, William James, in his *The Varieties of Religious Experience*, focused on mysticism as inner spiritual experiences that were essentially universal. He referred to these experiences as "pure consciousness events" that crossed the boundaries between different religions and their specific belief systems. James suggested that the people we call mystics merely describe their experiences after the event through the medium of whatever religious language is familiar to them. I noted that James's assumptions are seriously questioned these days. For example, the contemporary American philosopher Steven Katz asserts that mystics cannot have a preconscious, unmediated experience of God or of transcendent reality, however that is understood. No one can ever effectively separate experience from underlying frameworks of meaning and belief systems. Thus, the experiences of mystics are preformed by background beliefs that create the boundaries within which such experiences take place. In this chapter, I will explore the connections between mysticism and beliefs—mainly in relation to Christian theology but also with some references to similar connections in other religions.

Whatever we mean by the mystical dimension of religion, I believe that it subverts any temptation to become too dogmatic and pushes us into moving beyond what we can immediately grasp. Many of the issues I address are specific to the Western Christian theological tradition and its related spirituality. However, the Eastern Orthodox understanding of mystical theology continues to operate within an integrated patristic theological framework.

Interestingly, there is a contemporary increase of interest in mysticism in philosophical and theological circles, in part as a postmodern reaction against the notion of absolute metanarratives.[1] In the late twentieth century, a number of major Christian theologians, such as Karl Rahner and Rowan Williams, reengaged with the concept of mysticism and the mystical dimension of theology, in terms of a different way of knowing beyond a purely systematic theological method.[2] Because this way of knowing necessarily takes us beyond the boundaries of conceptual thinking and beyond conclusive definitions, there has been a renewed interest in what is known as the apophatic dimension of classical mystical theology. This places a strong emphasis on the impossibility of naming God as a "this" or a "that." The eminent British theologian Rowan Williams (also a former Archbishop of Canterbury) believes that this approach is in fact normative within the overall theological enterprise. As he puts it, "Apophasis is not a branch of theology, but an attitude which should undergird *all* theological discourse, and lead it towards the silence of contemplation and communion."[3] This view is reinforced by the journey of the

1. See Philip Sheldrake, *Spirituality and Theology: Christian Living and the Doctrine of God* (Maryknoll, NY: Orbis Books, 1998), especially 24–31.
2. See e.g., Karl Rahner, "The Theology of Mysticism," in *The Practice of Faith: A Handbook of Contemporary Spirituality*, ET, ed. K. Lehmann and L. Raffelt (New York: Crossroad, 1986), 70–77; Rowan Williams, *Teresa of Avila* (London: Geoffrey Chapman, 1991), chapter 5.
3. Rowan Williams, "The Via Negativa and the Foundations of Theology: An Introduction to the Thought of V. N. Lossky," in *New Studies in*

American Roman Catholic theologian, David Tracy, toward a belief that contemporary theologians must turn to the apophatic language of mystical writers in the current postmodern era. Tracy writes of the "uncanny negations" of mysticism as a form of theological release and, consciously aligning himself with Thomas Aquinas, suggests that intellectual silence may be "the final form of speech possible to any authentic speaker."[4]

UNION WITH THE TRANSCENDENT

As I suggested in the previous chapter, a word frequently used both by Christian mystics and by theological writers to describe the heart of mysticism is "union." However, in a more fundamental theological sense, union with God is the precondition of all human spiritual development rather than simply the most advanced stage. In addition, in nontheological studies of mysticism, union has sometimes been characterized in terms of passivity and by absorption into the divine where individual identity is lost. Apart from the difficulty of connecting this, without qualification, to theological understandings of how God relates to people in freedom and love, such a notion does not correspond to what we know of the great Christian mystics. On the contrary, the deep union with God reached by, for example, medieval mystical writers such as Bernard of Clairvaux, Francis of Assisi, or Catherine of Siena led them into greater activity and service on behalf of other people rather than the opposite. However, we cannot bypass entirely the ambiguity of some mystical language, particularly in the great fourteenth-century Rhineland mystic, the Dominican priest Meister Eckhart. Especially in his radically paradoxical vernacular German

---

Theology, vol. 1, ed. Stephen Sykes and Derek Holmes (London: Duckworth, 1980), 96.

4. See David Tracy, *The Analogical Imagination: Christian Theology and the Culture of Pluralism* (New York: Crossroad, 1991), 360, 385.

sermons, Eckhart appears to make daring assertions concerning the mystical identity between humans and God, which led to suspicions of heresy and the condemnation of some of Eckhart's teachings. However, at the same time, Eckhart preached that an absolute abyss separates us from a mysterious transcendent God. There is a necessary negation of all human concepts of "God" in our quest to reach out towards God's mysterious and transcendent *grunt* or "ground."[5]

Do We Give Priority to Interiority?

A second key theological theme related to mysticism is whether and to what degree we prioritize interiority within Christian mysticism. Interiority is not a straightforward concept. For Augustine and other early Church spiritual teachers, it did not imply the same thing as it might in our modern era. In his essay contribution to the multivolume *A History of Private Life*, Peter Brown reminds us that the earliest approaches to the Christian life inherited from late classical Judaism an intense sense of a vital solidarity between the individual person and the community. Individual human existence was intrinsically related to the common good. The perceived danger was that people might retreat into privacy rather than give themselves wholeheartedly to the task of serving their neighbors. Hence, Jewish writers turned their attention to the "thoughts of the heart"—the supposed core of human motivation and intention. Human destiny was a state of solidarity with others, expressed in the image of the undivided heart.[6]

5. See Bernard McGinn and Edmund Colledge, eds., *Meister Eckhart: The Essential Sermons, Commentaries, Treatises and Defense* (Mahwah, NJ: Paulist Press, 1985); and Bernard McGinn, ed., *Meister Eckhart: Teacher and Preacher* (Mahwah, NJ: Paulist Press, 1986).

6. See Peter Brown, "Late Antiquity," in *A History of Private Life*, vol. 1, ed. P. Vayne, *From Pagan Rome to Byzantium* (Cambridge, MA: Harvard University Press, 1996).

Following this tradition, the great theologian Augustine adopted the symbol of the heart as a way of expressing the essence of the human self. Augustine's language of the heart is not evidence of a privatized spirituality. What is interior to me is, for Augustine, where I am also united with the whole of creation. The *imago Dei* in which we are created and which is imprinted on the heart must be read alongside Augustine's doctrine of creation. In his *Commentary on Genesis*, Augustine suggests that Adam's sin was precisely to please himself and to live for himself (*secundum se vivere, sibi placere*). Thus, communion is ruptured—whether our union with God, our solidarity with other people, or our harmony with our own true self. In other words, sin is a withdrawal into self-centered privacy, which is quite different from interiority, according to Augustine. Self-seeking pride is the archetypal sin. Original Eden and the ideal City of God are both based on "the love that promotes the common good for the sake of the heavenly society" (*Commentary on Genesis*, XI.15.20). In fact, the most insidious sin was self-enclosed privacy. The private is seen as the opposite of common or public. For Augustine, the eternal Heavenly City will be the community in which there is the fullness of mutual sharing.[7] Within Augustine's theology there is a tension that should not be resolved between a striking sense of the personal self and an equally striking sense of the fundamentally social nature of human existence. "The heart" for Augustine is where a true integration of inner and outer existence, the spiritual and the embodied, happens. Equally, Augustine is clear that if anything is claimed to be in the heart or inside us but does not show itself outwardly in love and community, it is an illusion. In the words of a contemporary writer on Augustine, "The return to the heart is but the first

---

7. On this point, see Robert A. Markus, *The End of Ancient Christianity* (Cambridge: Cambridge University Press, 1998), 78.

step of a conversion process that proves itself in universal and unrestricted—catholic—love."[8]

MYSTICISM AND THE DOCTRINE OF GOD

When we address the question of the relationship between Christian theology and mysticism, there is one unavoidable starting point. Christians affirm that the meaning of human life and of all reality is judged in relation to a person—the Jewish teacher, Jesus of Nazareth, who lived in Roman-occupied Palestine during the early part of the first century CE. The story of Jesus of Nazareth is paradoxical. On the one hand, it portrays someone who existed in a quite specific time and place. However, these contingent realities were experienced by Jesus' early followers as universal in their implications. Jesus is "of Nazareth," the rabbi who is a carpenter's son. Yet, in the light of the Easter events, he is also known as "the Christ," the anointed one of God, the Savior of the world. The Christian community affirmed not simply that through the human Jesus, God speaks, but rather that the person of Jesus is God's incarnation.

Christian understandings of mysticism will always treat this understanding of Jesus as the basic reference point. What is vitally important is that this belief embodies a specific understanding of God and of God's self-disclosure. This understanding of God is sustained within a community of faith, that is, the church. Thus, our personal experiences, including mystical ones, are continually brought into conversation with this foundational story, with this original experience of the believing community and the many attempts across time to reflect upon it.

It is important to understand what Christian doctrines are really trying to express about God. The point of seeking doctrinal clarity (for example, in the early Christian era) is always to express, promote, and protect a quite distinctive *experience* of

---

8. Thomas Martin, *Our Restless Heart: The Augustinian Tradition* (London: Darton, Longman & Todd, 2003), 43.

God, along with its practical implications for everyday human life and for prayer. Authentic religious experiences, including mystical ones, in terms of a Christian understanding of revelation, are initiated by God and not simply by our subjective needs. As a result, they are challenging and profoundly disturbing.

The tradition of Christian spirituality attempts to respond to the question, "What kind of God do we have and what difference does it make to us?" The key doctrines formulated by the early Christian Church were those of God as Trinity and of Jesus Christ as truly God and truly human. All human statements about God have practical implications; we live what we affirm. In that sense, the tradition of Christian spirituality, including its mystical dimension of otherness, is an important test of the adequacy of human theologies of God that lie behind it. The Christian doctrine of God seeks to maintain a delicate balance between transcendence and immanence. This governs the way we understand and respond to creation and human embodiment. The classical heresies of the early Christian era were not considered unorthodox simply in terms of their technical language. Rather, they were seen as upsetting the delicate balance between transcendence and immanence with ultimately destructive results.

The language surrounding the traditional Christian belief in God's untouchable otherness (known as God's "impassability") derived largely from Greek philosophy. Plato's definition of perfection and Aristotle's idea of the creator as Unmoved Mover were especially influential. The language of impassability protects God's essential freedom. Yet it needs to be held in tension with biblical images of God's engagement with creation and with humanity. Otherwise, we would be left with a disconnected God who did not truly enter human history and who offered no final redemption for the human condition. Such a disconnection of God from creation is a short step from promoting a despotic God with whom there is no real communication and whose actions or demands are arbitrary and authoritarian.

Any individualistic approach to Christian spirituality and mysticism fails to reflect the communion of equal relationships that is God-in-Trinity. The nature of the Christian life was always an issue at the heart of early debates about the doctrine of God. To think of God as Trinity is fundamentally to assert, among other things, that within God there is society or relationship. To affirm that human beings are created in the image of that God implies that we are essentially social beings who are called to share more and more in the deep communion that is divine life itself. The crucial issue is the intimate link between the fundamental nature of God and God as revealed through creation and salvation.[9]

Approaches to spirituality and mysticism that are disengaged from the world rather than committed to it—and to its transformation—fail to reflect the irrevocable commitment of God to God's creation. This is what the doctrine of the incarnation seeks to express. Belief in the incarnation also invites people to adopt a balanced approach to human nature and especially to its material dimension, the body. This should be neither radically pessimistic nor naively optimistic. The incarnation is a governing principle of Christian living and of God's way of relating to creation and our way of response. This means that the Christian vision of God—and God's self-disclosure—forces our approaches to spirituality and mysticism to promote the fundamental importance of human material existence.

THEOLOGY IN PRACTICE

In Christianity, all theology—not merely spirituality and mysticism—is practical in the sense that it needs to be practiced. In the context of academic theology, this viewpoint suggests that what is conventionally called "applied" or "prac-

9. See, e.g., Anthony Meredith, "Patristic Spirituality," in *Companion Encyclopedia of Theology*, ed. P. Byrne and L. Houlden (London: Routledge, 1995), 536–57.

tical" theology is not an optional extra. However, the place of "practice" in theology means more than a specialist field. Theology as a whole is not merely concerned with content and specific resources. For the Christian theologian, personal faith is an irreducible horizon that is present at every moment of experiencing and interpreting theology.[10] Thus, to "do" theology means to become a "theological person" rather than merely using theological tools.

The point is that being a "theological person" is more than a purely intellectual exercise. The ancient concept of *theologia* is much broader. It inevitably involves what Eastern Christianity has called *theoria*. At first sight, this word is misleading to Western eyes. *Theoria* is more accurately translated as "contemplation" rather than "theory."[11] The committed believer is one who *lives* theology rather than "does" it as an activity detached from who she or he is. Sadly, there is still a tendency in Western thought to think and act as if "knowledge" meant something purely objective and rational. However, theology in its richest sense is essentially performative as well as informative. It is concerned with action as well as with ideas. "Being a theologian" involves a quality of presence to the reality we reflect upon (God) as much as a concern for the techniques of a specific discipline.

The ancient meaning of a theologian as a person who sees and experiences the content of theological reflection connects well with contemporary understandings of the self-implicating nature of theology. Theology, spirituality, and mysticism in their fullest senses are all self-implicating. This does not imply

---

10. On the relation of practice to the theological enterprise, see, e.g., David Tracy, *The Analogical Imagination: Christian Theology and The Culture of Pluralism* (New York: Crossroad, 1991), chapter 2, "A Theological Portrait of the Theologian."

11. See John Meyendorff, *Byzantine Theology* (New York: Fordham University Press, 1979), introduction; also Vladimir Lossky, *The Mystical Theology of the Eastern Church*, rev. ed. (London: James Clarke, 1991), chapter 1.

anti-intellectualism. However, while critical analysis may be
the servant of good theology, it is not why we do theology. A
kind of transformation is implied by the search for knowledge.
In the words of David Tracy, " 'Saying the truth' is distinct
from, although never separate from, 'doing the truth.' . . .
More concretely, there is never an authentic disclosure of truth
which is not also transformative."[12]

Mysticism and a Theology of Unknowing

One of the most fundamental aspects of the Christian understanding of God is that human relationships with God embrace
a paradox of knowing and not-knowing. This has particular
force in the context of mysticism and with a conversation not
only between spirituality and theology but also between the
Christian tradition as a whole and contemporary culture.

The history of Christianity is often presented purely in terms
of ever greater doctrinal refinement and definition. However,
Christianity has always affirmed that God is beyond the capacity of anyone to define completely or finally to know. One
striking New Testament image is the story of Peter's vision
before his visit to Cornelius and his family as described in the
book of Acts, chapter 10. As an observant Jew, Peter "knew"
what God wanted in terms of dietary laws. However, in the
vision at Caesarea, he was challenged to eat what Jewish law
declared to be profane and unclean. When Peter queried this,
he heard a voice say, "What God has made clean, you must
not call profane." In visiting the "unclean" Gentile, Cornelius,
Peter made an important connection. He came to realize that
with God there are no favorites and that God is as much the
God of the Gentiles as of the Jewish people. According to the
story, God profoundly challenged Peter's assumptions about
where God was to be found and how God acts. This point is
most strikingly underlined by the detail that Cornelius and

his family received the Holy Spirit even though they were not baptized (Acts 10:44-48). The story also affirms the power of God's Spirit to blow where it wills and so to lead us into all truth. Throughout its history, Christianity has struggled with its discomfort at the wild and disruptive side of God and with the unpredictability of God's way of leading.

Human attempts to think about God seek a balance between striving for images of God and a recognition that the reality of God is ultimately beyond all images. The words kataphatic (positive) and apophatic (negative) have classically been used to describe the two dimensions of human relations with God. The kataphatic element emphasizes the way of creating images of God. It is a positive theology, a theology of affirmation based on a high doctrine of creation and of human life as contexts for God's self-revelation. In contrast, the apophatic element emphasizes not-knowing: silence, darkness, passivity (to a degree), and the absence of imagery. It is a negative theology in the sense of being a theology of denial. A sixth-century Eastern Christian writer known as pseudo-Dionysius was one of the most influential exponents of the concepts of apophatic and kataphatic theologies.[13] He had a major impact on Western mystical thought.

In pseudo-Dionysius's approach to God, knowing and unknowing are mutually related rather than mutually exclusive. The whole of creation is brought into being by God to show

13. On the broader context of patristic theology, see Jaroslav Pelikan, *Christianity and Classical Culture* (New Haven: Yale University Press, 1993), chapter 4, "God and the Ways of Knowing."

The complete works of pseudo-Dionysius are now available in reliable English translation. See Colm Luibheid and Paul Rorem, eds., *Pseudo-Dionysius: The Complete Works* (Mahwah, NJ: Paulist Press, 1987). For useful studies of pseudo-Dionysius, see Andrew Louth, *The Origins of the Christian Mystical Tradition* (Oxford: Oxford University Press, 1981), chapter VIII, and his *Denys the Areopagite* (London: Chapman, 1989); also Denys Turner, *The Darkness of God: Negativity in Christian Mysticism* (Cambridge: Cambridge University Press, 1995), chapter 2.

forth divine glory. The cosmos is to be viewed positively as the self-revelation of God's goodness. "Good" is, therefore, the first affirmation (or image) of God discussed by pseudo-Dionysius. Again, in pseudo-Dionysius's theology, the Trinity is first realized in terms of distinctions between the "persons" of the Trinity, Father, Son, and Holy Spirit, whereby we can know something of God. However, underlying these distinctions or contained within them is a unity or synthesis that we cannot ultimately comprehend. Therefore, the theology of the Trinity is a way of knowing because it seeks to affirm something about God. Yet, at the same time, it is a way of unknowing because the affirmations we make immediately push us beyond what we can ultimately grasp. Paradoxically, the doctrine of the Trinity both reveals God and yet reveals God as beyond human knowing. Through our relationship with God as revealed in creation and in the midst of our affirmations, we come to realize that God never becomes our possession or an object of rational knowledge.

To seek God through images prevents us from losing touch with God's communication with us in and through creation, through our own lives and via the incarnation. Created material reality is not a distraction from which God is utterly removed. Yet we cannot reduce God to human categories. God has always received many names and yet always remains beyond every name. Indeed, the apparently endless "naming" of God finally draws us back into the mysterious divine depths beyond the limitations of naming, reason, and subjective experience. Difficult though it may be, the Christian tradition suggests that we must hold in creative tension the process of imaging God and the process of denial that any image actually *is* God. For some people, apophatic or negative theology is ultimately normative. This is because the apophatic way should not be seen simply as a way of correcting an unbalanced "positive" theology.

It is interesting that a number of contemporary analyses of the implications for Christian spirituality of postmodern experience reflect these central paradoxes in the doctrine of God. It is true that one aspect of postmodernism highlights "fragmentation." However, the recipe for recovery points toward rather than undermines a fuller appreciation of the riches of the Christian doctrine of God. We may now realize once again that the world is ultimately incalculable and beyond the laws of the human mind. This is not necessarily a recipe for despair. It opens the possibility of a return to wonder and worship at the heart of theology and our approaches to spirituality and mysticism.

One recent analysis of spirituality in a postmodern context speaks of a number of crucial needs that relate directly to the doctrine of God. Spirituality must be strongly incarnational and engaged with the ordinariness of material existence. It should emphasize the existential quality of God's relationship to us and encourage a radical belief in the unconditional love of God behind all material reality and human experience. The cross is the suffering of God within human suffering. Some postmodernist writing (for example, by the French philosopher Jacques Derrida) has been described as a form of apophatic or "negative theology."[14] Whether or not this is appropriate, contemporary theology and spirituality certainly need to reflect upon the tradition of the hiddenness of God in the context of the absence of God in the lives of many contemporary people. This sense of the hiddenness of God may help to purify our false, overly dogmatic images of God.

The hidden face of God plays a particularly strong role in the Christian tradition of mysticism. The believer is brought to the frontiers of language or conceptual thinking and to the edge of mystery—a Mystery which is, nevertheless, intensely present. It is not surprising that the great French Jesuit scholar of mysticism, Michel de Certeau, draws parallels between postmodern

14. Rowan Williams, "Hegel and the Gods of Postmodernity," in *Shadow of Spirit: Postmodernism and Religion*, ed. P. Byrne and L. Houlden (London: Routledge, 1992), 73–80.

culture and the mystical tradition. Both the mystic and the postmodern person live in a kind of movement of perpetual departure. In the words of de Certeau, they are both wanderers and pilgrims lost in "the totality of the immense." Each of them "with the certainty of what is lacking, knows of every place and object that it is *not that*, one cannot stay *there* nor be content with *that*."[15]

Modernity placed a powerful emphasis on intelligibility, not least in relation to language about God. Because of this, those people whose lives affirm the essential otherness of a mysterious God are described by de Certeau as outsiders to what he called "the Modern project."[16] Echoing de Certeau, the American Catholic theologian David Tracy suggests that hope lies particularly in the challenge to traditional power and privilege offered by an otherness that is present in marginal groups. He points particularly to the mystics and the mad.[17] Perhaps this is why de Certeau was fascinated throughout his writings by the seventeenth-century Jesuit mystic Jean-Joseph Surin (whom de Certeau called "my guardian"). Surin was for many years also profoundly disturbed psychologically and consequently isolated and oppressed.[18] I will mention de Certeau again in chapter 6 and briefly explore his overall thinking about mysticism in the conclusion to this book.

At present, there is a great curiosity about mysticism in Western culture. This is a recognizable part of postmodern religiosity. It seems to express a desire for an immediacy of

15. Michel de Certeau, *The Mystic Fable*, vol. 1, ET (Chicago: University of Chicago Press, 1992), 299. The emphases are the author's.

16. De Certeau, *Mystic Fable*, especially "Introduction," 1–26.

17. David Tracy, *On Naming the Present: God, Hermeneutics, and Church* (Maryknoll, NY: Orbis Books, 1994), 3–6.

18. See *Mystic Fable*, passim but especially chapter 7, "The Enlightened Illiterate." De Certeau also edited the work of Surin: *Jean-Joseph Surin: Correspondence* (Paris: Desclée, 1963) and *Jean-Joseph Surin: Guide spirituel pour la perfection* (Paris: Desclée, 1963).

presence to the spiritual and the transcendent. This is presumed to be beyond what is thought of as the cold objectivity of the life and teachings of the institutional church.[19] Mystics of every age believed that the way to true understanding and fulfilment is the way of unknowing and dispossession. In the words of the sixteenth-century Spanish mystic John of the Cross:

> To reach satisfaction in all
>   desire its possession in nothing.
> To come to possess all
>   desire the possession of nothing.
> To arrive at being all
>   desire to be nothing.
> To come to the knowledge of all
>   desire the knowledge of nothing.[20]

The postmodern affirmation that all religious language is relative reminds us that religious definitions are necessarily provisional. The reality we name as "God" exists beyond all human categories—even beyond the familiar category of Being.[21] It is a central belief of mystical Christianity that God is not intelligible and cannot be known in terms of rational thinking. Yet, as mystics of every age have intuitively grasped,

---

19. See, e.g., Carlo Carozza, "Mysticism and the Crisis of Religious Institutions," in *Mysticism and the Institutional Crisis*, ed. Christian Duquoc and Gustavo Gutierrez, in *Concilium* 4 (1994): 17–26. However, in an important and complex study, Denys Turner questions the modern experiential concept of "mysticism." He suggests that the apophatic tradition did not expound subjective mysticism in this sense. See Turner, *Darkness of God*, introduction and chapter 11, "From Mystical Theology to Mysticism."

20. John of the Cross, *The Ascent of Mount Carmel*, Book 1, chapter 13, no. 11, in *The Collected Works of St. John of the Cross*, ed. Kieran Kavanaugh and Otilio Rodriguez (Washington, DC: Institute of Carmelite Studies, 1979).

21. On God and the category of Being, see Jean-Luc Marion, *God without Being*, ET (Chicago: University of Chicago Press, 1995), especially chapter 3.

the God-Who-Is-Love may be touched existentially in our desiring and in longing love. In the words of the anonymous fourteenth-century English mystical text, *The Cloud of Unknowing:*

> Now all rational creatures, angels and men alike, have in them, each one individually, one chief working power which is called a knowing power, and another chief working power called a loving power; and of these two powers, God, who is the maker of them, is always incomprehensible to the first, the knowing power. But to the second, which is the loving power, he is entirely comprehensible. . . .

> No man can think of God himself. Therefore, it is my wish to leave everything that I can think of and choose for my love the thing I cannot think. Because [God] can certainly be loved but not thought. (*The Cloud of Unknowing*, chapters IV and VI)[22]

This dynamic love that exists at the center of our being and which is in a perpetual search for fulfilment is, as many mystics teach, also the very heart of the mystery of God-as-Trinity. The seventeenth-century Anglican spiritual writer and poet Thomas Traherne suggests that desire or "wants" lie at the heart of God.

> This is very strange that God should want. For in Him is the fullness of all Blessedness: He overflowed eternally. His wants are as glorious as infinite: perfective needs that are in His nature and ever Blessed because always satisfied. He is from eternity full of want, or else He would not be full of Treasure. Infinite want is the very ground and cause of infinite Treasure. It is incredible, yet very

22. See James Walsh, ed., *The Cloud of Unknowing* (Mahwah, NJ: Paulist Press, 1981), chapter IV and chapter VI.

plain. Want is the fountain of all His fullness. (*Centuries of Meditation*)[23]

It is worth noting that a number of modern theologians have been fascinated by the theological possibilities of mystical writings. David Tracy, for example, suggests that in our postmodern era "we may now learn to drop earlier dismissals of 'mysticism' and allow its uncanny negations to release us."[24] This reflects Tracy's own journey toward a belief that the apophatic language of the mystics is where theologians must turn in our present times.

> As critical and speculative philosophical theologians and artists learn to let go into the sensed reality of some event of manifestation, some experience of releasement and primal thinking, a sense of the reality of mystical experience can begin to show itself in itself. Even those with no explicit mystical experience, like myself, sense that thinking can become thanking, that silence does become, even for an Aquinas when he would "write no more," the final form of speech possible to any authentic speaker.[25]

Karl Rahner and Rowan Williams have both reminded us that mysticism is integral to the theological enterprise. Because it cannot be reduced to subjective affectivity, mysticism points toward another way of knowing and learning. In fact, the key to good theology is prayer, understood in its fullest sense as a relationship with, or contemplation of, God rather than simply performing devotions and techniques of meditation.

---

23. Thomas Traherne, *Centuries* (Oxford: Mowbray, 1975), 1.42. Traherne was one of the so-called "Caroline Divines" living in the mid-seventeenth century. An Anglican priest and arguably a mystic, many of his most striking spiritual works have only been recovered in recent decades.
24. Tracy, *Analogical Imagination*, 360.
25. Tracy, 385.

Perhaps we may go further still and say that all true prayer is true theology and vice versa. For true prayer and true theology are both matters of the heart and the head. They each point to a unity of love and knowledge beyond traditional post-Enlightenment thought.

In the West, we have inherited a tendency to believe that knowledge means only abstract intelligence and objective analysis. The problem with theological knowledge is that while we may be impelled to speak of God, we cannot in the end speak definitively *about* God in the sense of capturing God's essence. The problem with a purely intellectual search for God is that it necessarily regards what is sought as an object or an objective that can be reached. In Christian terms, insofar as we can speak of the human search for God, it will be a search that involves a continuous failure to capture God in any final sense. Thus, the patristic mystical theologian Gregory of Nyssa could suggest that a "true" vision of God involves a perpetual movement onward—even, arguably, when we reach what we refer to as "heaven."

> This truly is the vision of God: never to be satisfied in the desire to see him. But one must always, by looking at what he can see, rekindle his desire to see more. Thus, no limit would interrupt growth in the ascent to God, since no limit to the Good can be found nor is the increasing of desire for the Good brought to an end because it is satisfied.[26]

MYSTICISM AND BELIEF IN WORLD RELIGIONS

Arguably, among the major world religions, Christianity has developed the most complicated and carefully structured belief system—embraced by "theology." Writers about other

26. See the modern English translation of Gregory of Nyssa, *The Life of Moses*, ed. Everett Ferguson, trans. Abraham Malherbe, Classics of Western Spirituality (Mahwah, NJ: Paulist, 1978), Book 2.239.

religions also sometimes use the term "theology," even though the word has Christian origins. It derives from ancient Greek and then Latin words meaning "sayings" or "reasoning" about God. However, as in Christianity, mysticism in other religions cannot be separated from their foundational beliefs.[27]

First of all, I want to summarize mystical aspects of the other two Abrahamic religions, Judaism and Islam. As we shall see in later chapters, the mystical dimensions of Judaism are closely linked to everyday Jewish religious life and to ethics. However, these in turn are expressions of religious belief embraced by the Torah. Life concerns more than the material world, and this "more" is to be understood as a personal God. God is Creator who is in a covenant relationship with humans (notably, the Jewish people) who are believed to have an inherent spiritual dimension (the soul) that is in conversation with God. One of the best-known expressions of Jewish mysticism is known as Kabbalah. This embraces teachings that seek to explain the intimate relationship between an eternal and indefinable God and humanity. What may be called the "mystical theology" of the Kabbalah teaches the inner meaning of the Scriptures, of later rabbinical writings, and of Jewish religious observance. The "unperceived" is actually the truly "real." The concept of *sefiroth* in Kabbalism stands for manifestations or emanations of God which channel the divine life force and the unknowable divine essence to the world of creation and of human life.

Islamic mysticism is best known through the tradition called Sufism. The fact that, at various times in history, Sufism also

27. I have written briefly elsewhere about the mystical dimensions of other religions and also of esoteric movements such as Theosophy and Rosicrucianism. See Philip Sheldrake, *Spirituality: A Very Short Introduction* (Oxford: Oxford University Press, 2012), chapter 3, "Spirituality and Experience"; see also Philip Sheldrake, *Spirituality: A Guide for the Perplexed* (London: Bloomsbury, 2014), part 2, chapters 5–9 passim.

had a definable influence on both Judaism and Christianity underlines its predominantly devotional, practical, and expressive nature (not least through poetry, music, and dance) rather than a narrow emphasis on Islamic beliefs or on intellectual knowledge. Nevertheless, the sayings of Islamic mystics are implicitly based on two key aspects of Islamic theology. For example, in what can be thought of as the spiritual theology of Ibn Arabi, born in Murcia in Spain during the late twelfth century, *tawhid*—or the unity of God—and *dhikr*—or recalling the names of God—are two key themes. Disciples need to be purified in their inner selves so that they may be united with God's all-encompassing presence. In some Sufi teachings there is also the concept that the spiritual journey has different stages. These spiritual stages parallel similar theories in Christian mystical theology. This Sufi concept of stages sometimes involved teaching about *fana* or spiritual annihilation. According to this teaching, if a Sufi practitioner was purified of material desire and was then lost in the love of God, the person's ego and individual will are somehow annihilated so that he or she is able to dwell solely in God and only for God. Some Sufi teachers went as far as to say that there is then a kind of absorption into the divine life. However, another important Sufi, al-Ghazali (died c1111 CE), rejected any literal understanding of human annihilation and of being absorbed into God because he believed that this was incompatible with Islamic theistic orthodoxy.

Turning to Hinduism, this is the most perplexing of the world religions because there is no single agreed belief system but a plurality of understandings of God, the material world, and human nature. The most intellectual version is the Vedantic religion based on the speculative thought of the Upanishads. Some, but not all, Hindu religious philosophies are theistic—that is, there is a divine reality who created the cosmos and sustains it. Depending on one's Hindu sect, the divine may be a single supreme God (monotheism), a variety of Gods (polytheism), or a sense that all reality is somehow divine (pantheism). However, it has been argued that behind the many Hindu deities lies a single supreme divine spirit. There is an explicitly theistic frame of belief in the scriptural text, the Bhagavad Gita. However, overall, Hinduism is more a religion of ascetical movements and ritual practices. The well-known concept of a cycle of birth, death, and rebirth (*samsara*) has a strongly ethical basis as it relates to our deeds and behavior in the present life (*karma*). For some nondualist Hindus, our human spirit is ultimately united to the supreme soul (Brahman). The goal of human life may be thought of in quasi-mystical terms as realizing this profound identity between the human self and the supreme soul, thereby reaching a state of freedom from the recurring cycle of birth, death, and rebirth. This state of *moksha* implies enlightenment, freedom from ignorance, self-realization, self-actualization, and liberation. With the arrival of Western thought in India under the British Raj, this became associated with the essentially Western concept of "mysticism."

Finally, in Buddhism "mysticism" relates to fundamental background teachings. Despite some misunderstandings, these teachings are agnostic rather than dogmatically atheistic in terms of the existence of a God or gods. However, what seems clear is that the Buddha denied that we are dependent on any God to "save" us. Therefore, the basis of Buddhist mysticism is not an intimate relationship with a personal God. What are essential in Buddhism are the teachings about the spiritual path and spiritual practice. These teachings may be summarized as the famous Four Noble Truths: first, the pervasive reality of suffering; second, material craving as the cause of human suffering; third, the possibility of overcoming this suffering by true understanding and proper discipline; and finally, pursuing an Eightfold Path toward the extinction of suffering and the attainment of ultimate liberation and enlightenment in *nirvāna*. This Eightfold Path involves right understanding;

becoming free from craving; cultivating right speech free from malice; pursuing right action by avoiding all misconduct; right living; right effort by striving to purify ourselves from evil thoughts; right mindfulness by being properly aware of the nature of one's body and mind; and lastly, right concentration through the practice of meditation. Because an unavoidable aspect of worldly existence is impermanence, a key element of the Buddhist mystical path is achieving nonattachment to material reality. Nonattachment also relates to the way we understand the true self. The Buddhist mystical path is a process of moving from self-preoccupation and an egocentric life to embrace the "no-self." Thus, *nirvāna* is the ultimate extinction of suffering in a state of tranquility where the independent self is recognized as an illusory aspect of worldly existence. In the Japanese Zen tradition of Buddhism, finding the "Buddha nature" (the noblest qualities we possess) is particularly associated with meditative practice as the path to self-realization. The key is that true enlightenment comes about, not through intellectual reasoning, but through the practice of meditation, self-imposed discipline, and ethical behavior.

CONCLUSION

In conclusion, from a Christian perspective we cannot separate our attempts to speak of God and our desire to live spiritually. At first sight this does not appear to sit easily with a tendency in modern Western culture to separate spirituality and mysticism from any system of religious belief or from a commitment to traditional religious groups, such as the Christian church. As we have seen, there is also a suspicion of what are sometimes called "metanarratives" or complete and exclusive systems of thought that claim to explain the meaning of life. Yet none of the world religions, not least Christianity, can escape from their fundamental frameworks of belief. These frameworks are expressed in Christianity by affirming God-as-Trinity and God's incarnation in the person of Jesus of Nazareth. They act as the boundaries within which we come to understand ourselves, other people, and the world around us. In that sense, the Christian story of God revealed in the person of Jesus is a narrative that offers an explanation for the meaning of existence.

Having said this, the Christian mystical tradition reminds us, importantly, that the language we use about God is always provisional. Historically, the Christian way of understanding reality has always sought a balance between the desire to speak about God (the affirmative or kataphatic way) and the need to recognize that God is ultimately beyond all human definitions (the negative or apophatic way). This elusive aspect of God has been best expressed in the traditions of mysticism and spirituality. The path of spirituality and mysticism reminds us that true "knowledge" of God is a matter of the heart as much as of the head.

Part Two of this book will now explore five different approaches to the mystical journey. These will be illustrated by material drawn from a range of world religions as well as from Christianity and, where relevant, from aspects of some esoteric movements which claim to espouse certain mystical principles.

part
two

Five Dimensions
of Mysticism

CHAPTER THREE

LOVE AND DESIRE

The theme of love, desire, and longing is a powerful one in mystical writings both in Christianity and in other religious traditions. Some mystics emphasize the ecstatic nature of love and desire. Our deepest longing and desire reflect God's own powerful longing within us. This has the potential to lead us to an intimate encounter with God. The Song of Songs in the Jewish Scriptures had an extensive influence on Christian mystical writings. The book is a collection of powerful love poems spoken alternately by a woman and a man. In both Jewish and Christian writers, this was interpreted allegorically as expressing the passion of divine-human love. The themes of love and desire also appear in the "bridal mysticism" of such medieval women writers as the Beguines (for example Hadewijch) and in the fourteenth-century English mystic Julian of Norwich. Later, the theme is powerfully expressed in the writings of the sixteenth-century Spanish Carmelites, Teresa of Avila and John of the Cross. Wants, desires, and longing are also present in the seventeenth-century Anglican mystic and spiritual writer Thomas Traherne, as well as in the outstanding poetry of George Herbert. Beyond Christianity, love and desire is a powerful theme in the two Jewish mystical traditions of Kabbalah and Hasidism. The theme also appears in Islam, notably in Sufi mysticism—for example, in the poetry of Rumi. Finally, and more controversially, the motif of longing appears in the twentieth-century Dutch Jewish writer Etty Hillesum, who died in Auschwitz and came from a nonreligious Jewish family. However, over time Etty entered into an unconventional but deep spiritual journey that is described in her diaries and letters. Etty's restless longing as well as intense spiritual passion, while detached from formal religion, gave a profoundly mystical tone to her writings. In particular, this led her to an encounter with what she called "the God within."

What Is Desire?

The power of desire in our lives is inescapable and, in its deepest sense, is a God-given dimension of human existence. Deep desire is what drives all human spirituality. However, in Christianity and other faiths, spirituality is concerned with how we focus our desires. Christian spirituality is clear that our restless longing can ultimately only be satisfied by God. In other words, our deep desire is infinite in its potential. It pushes us beyond the limitations of the present moment to reach out toward a future that is beyond our ability to describe, let alone control. This is why the greatest teachers of Christian mysticism were so concerned with God-driven desire and how we are to understand and direct it.

Our desires unavoidably overlap with our neediness. This is why it is vital to distinguish between superficial "wants" and our deepest desire. If we reflect carefully on our lives, we may come to understand more clearly how unconscious needs have a capacity to make us behave in ways that fail to express our deepest self. For example, we may be driven by a need to succeed, including spiritually, and also a need to be seen as successful! When we think more deeply about our deep desires rather than needs, we sense that true desire moves us to reach out to something or someone that speaks to us of ultimate meaning. Such a movement highlights the deeper questions of identity and purpose.

The fourteenth-century Italian mystic Catherine of Siena recognized the positive and extraordinary power of our desires when she wrote that deep desire is one of the few ways of touching God because "you have nothing infinite except your soul's love and desire."[1] Meister Eckhart, a Rhineland Dominican and mystic of the same period, suggested that the reason why we are not able to see God clearly is the faintness of our desire. The language of desire also permeates the Church of England's sixteenth-century *Book of Common Prayer*, one of the foundational documents of the English Reformation. In the language of Archbishop Cranmer, we need to distinguish between following "too much the devices and desires of our own hearts" and seeking the "holy desires," "good counsels," and "just works" that proceed only from God's inner inspiration. "Holy desires" ultimately find their rest and fulfilment only in God.

The sensual quality (understood properly) of such holy desires is apparent in the language used by many of the greatest Christian mystics. The problem is that conventional Christian approaches to a "spiritual life" have too often taught people to believe that the spiritual life mainly concerns self-denial. This made it difficult for Christians to engage with life in a passionate way. On the other hand, attention to our deepest desire cultivates within us a capacity for passionate engagement. There is always a degree of risk in focusing on desire because ill-directed desire dissipates our energies. However, our deepest desire also generates power and energy to galvanize our spirituality.

In the Christian Scriptures, God's Spirit blows where it wills. This is the risky, wild side of God that impels us to pour ourselves out into situations, commitments, and relationships.

---

1. See Susan Noffke, ed., *Catherine of Siena, The Dialogue* (Mahwah, NJ: Paulist Press, 1980), 270.

The Spirit of God is vulnerable as well as powerful. God's Spirit does not simply "lead us into all truth" but also leads us into the vulnerability of the way of Jesus. However, at the same time, by taking such risks, we learn that we are protected securely at some deep level beyond our own capacities. The Spirit is the power of God within the lives of each of us which truly sustains us.

DESIRE IN SCRIPTURE

Behind the Christian Scriptures lie the Jewish Scriptures, known to Christians as the Old Testament. These have played a significant role throughout the history of Christian spirituality across two thousand years. As already noted, a particularly influential text in Christian mystical writings is the Song of Songs. Its direct use of erotic imagery found special favor with a range of Christian writers from Origen to Bernard of Clairvaux and other medieval Cistercians, the Beguines, and women mystics of all kinds. In these mystical writers, there was frequently a combination of an ascetical lifestyle and deep expressions of human emotions in poetry and hymns. The highly personal language of the Song of Songs made it a powerful expression of God's relationship with the Christian community and also with individuals. The acceptance of the Song of Songs into the canon of Christian Scripture, despite some theological misgivings, legitimized *eros* love as a way of describing the relationship between God and human beings.

For example, the early Christian theologian Origen was quite emphatic in his writings in using the word *eros* for the love relationship between God and humanity rather than the more respectable *agape*. Origen was effectively the foundation of an extraordinary genre of Christian literature. Across time, the many Christian writings on the Song of Songs translated human passion, poetically expressed, into a complex allegory of the mystical quest for union with God the Beloved.

The Western European Middle Ages saw a particular flowering of the language of desire, love, and mystical marriage in spiritual writings. An important example was the monastic reform movement known as the Cistercians, which emerged in the twelfth century and produced one of the most important medieval traditions of spirituality. The Cistercian reform was a purification of the Benedictine monastic tradition through returning to a stricter observance of the Rule of St. Benedict. However, the spiritual ethos of the Cistercians was also the product of new cultural movements during the twelfth century. This period became known as "the century of love" in both religious and everyday contexts.

The Cistercians produced an important body of spiritual writing, such as the treatises, homilies, and letters of Bernard of Clairvaux. His work was a classic expression of mystical-contemplative responses to Scripture. This contrasted with the more philosophical tone of the emerging "new theology" in the cathedral schools and early universities. In tune with the overall spirit of the times, Bernard of Clairvaux promoted an optimistic view of human nature and particularly of the human capacity for God. One of Bernard's most famous expressions of mystical theology is his *Sermons on the Song of Songs*.[2] Other Cistercians, such as William of St. Thierry and the English monks Gilbert of Hoyland and John of Ford, continued the tradition of spiritual commentaries on the Song of Songs. This became a hallmark of Cistercian spirituality. Interestingly, some post-Reformation Protestants were influenced by Cistercian spirituality. A notable example was the seventeenth-century English Puritan writer, Isaac Ambrose, who explicitly cited Bernard of Clairvaux and drew upon the Cistercian tradition of sermons on the Song of Songs.

2. For translations of, and an introduction to, Bernard's writings, see G. R. Evans, ed., *Bernard of Clairvaux: Selected Works*, Classics of Western Spirituality (Mahwah, NJ: Paulist Press, 1987).

As I will explain later, the sixteenth-century Carmelite reformers and important spiritual writers Teresa of Avila and John of the Cross were also strongly influenced by the book of the Song of Songs and by the concept of spiritual marriage.

Bridal Mysticism

The concept of spiritual marriage brings me to an important medieval example of love mysticism, widely known as Bridal Mysticism, also influenced by the Song of Songs. A well-known example is the movement called the Beguines. This was a lay spiritual movement of women which emerged towards the end of the twelfth century as part of the new city developments in Northern Europe, especially in what are now Belgium and the Netherlands. The Beguines were not monastic but were involved in charitable work, spiritual teaching, and even preaching.[3]

The mysterious figure of Hadewijch is a classic example of the mystical strand of Beguine spirituality. We know very little about her apart from the fact that she was Flemish and was probably writing in the first part of the thirteenth century. From the surviving writings, it appears that Hadewijch was well educated and familiar with the literary tradition of courtly love lyrics. Her undoubted writings include forty-five poems in stanzas, sixteen poems in couplets, thirty-one letters (both letters of spiritual guidance and mini-treatises), and fourteen visions. Like Julian of Norwich, her writings are not systematic but pursue three fundamental themes of which the most important is that of love—both as God's own nature and as the ideal human response to God. The theme of love appears

---

3. For an overview of the Beguines and their spirituality, see, e.g., Saskia Murk-Jansen, *Brides in the Desert: The Spirituality of the Beguines,* ed. Philip Sheldrake, Traditions of Christian Spirituality (Maryknoll, NY: Orbis Books, 1998).

most prominently in Hadewijch's poetry. She suggests that
we can only touch God through love. Hadewijch expresses
this in the language of a human courtly lover relating to a
highborn mistress (who is God).[4] She notes that it is painful
that our deepest desires are never finally satisfied. In her visions, Hadewijch experienced Jesus Christ speaking to her of
"painful desire" and the "privation of what you desire above
all . . . this reaching out to me who am unreachable" (*The
Complete Works*, 283). Hadewijch talks about the unquiet
nature of desire in one of her poems in couplets (number 10),
"Not Feeling but Love." In our "childish" love we sometimes
want to be satisfied with "many particular things" because we
mistake the "delight" of good feelings for true "desire." In
Hadewijch's experience, this would be to settle for something
that is less than we are called to by God.

> Not for feeling's sake must we learn to serve,
> But only to love with love in Love.

For Hadewijch, in order to encounter the unreachable God
who is Love, we need to love without rest and "desire above
measure"—that is, beyond reason. So our spirit, even

> when it feels misery,
> It can learn to know Love's mode of action.

The effect of divine Love in us is that,

> The proximity of the nature of Love
> Deprives the soul of its rest:
> The more Love comes, the more she steals.

4. See Columba Hart, ed., *Hadewijch—The Complete Works* (Mahwah,
NJ: Paulist Press, 1980).

To those who really seek to live riskily in Love and who enter what Hadewijch calls the divine "abyss," Love "gives an unquiet life." Why is this? It is because divine Love "causes hearts, in Love, to be in constant striving."

> Desires of love, moreover, cannot
> By all these explanations be quieted.
> Desire strives in all things for more than it possesses:
> Love does not allow it to have any rest.

In a daring statement (also present in her Letter 8 and in her Vision 13), Hadewijch suggests that a "noble unfaith" is higher than "fidelity." While "fidelity" is related to reason and "often lets desire be satisfied," unfaith "never allows desire any rest in any fidelity." This "unfaith" is difficult to define. However, it is perhaps best understood as an experience of living in the absence of consoling feelings. It is the opposite of an experience of peaceful rest that settles for something less than everything. "Unfaith" turns our human spirit away from taking pleasure merely "in what it has in hand." "Unfaith" is suspicious of any sense that divine Love is something that can somehow be grasped or possessed. Thus, at the very heart of Hadewijch's spirituality of love is the total otherness of God. The moment you feel yourself to be in guaranteed contact with God, you have missed God. Hadewijch's "unfaith" bypasses what we can control. For Hadewijch, there is a painful quality to all true love. This is because it is ultimately there for the sake of love in itself rather than for feelings of satisfaction. If we ever find ourselves continuing to love "beyond the immediate facts" in a relationship with someone else, we have an inkling of what Hadewijch understands about our love relationship with God.

I will discuss the importance of the medieval Rhineland Dominican theologian, Meister Eckhart, in the next chapter on "Knowing and Unknowing." However, Eckhart also explored the notion of God's desire, which implies that, in some sense, God needs us. As we shall see in a moment, the same paradoxical idea of God's "need" appears in the writings of the fourteenth-century English woman mystic, Julian of Norwich. God's "need" is a difficult notion for Christians to understand. In one of his most direct and radical statements about God's love of humanity, Meister Eckhart preached:

> Know that God loves the soul so powerfully that it stag-
> gers the mind. If one were to deprive God of this so that
> he did not love the soul, one would deprive him of his
> life and being, or one would kill God if we may say such
> a thing. For that same love by which God loves the soul
> is his life, and in this same love the Holy Spirit blossoms
> forth; and this same love *is* the Holy Spirit.[5]

Henry Suso, one of Eckhart's Dominican followers (along with Johannes Tauler), is the most literary of the Rhineland trio of mystical writers. Suso left many treatises, letters, and sermons, as well as an autobiography. Suso may be thought of as a theological mystic like Eckhart, directly influenced by Eckhart's ideas on negativity and on union with God. How-ever, Suso also offered a very different spirituality in his *Little Book of Eternal Wisdom*. Here there are strong echoes of love mysticism and Christ-centered devotion. This work became a devotional classic.[6]

Another major medieval mystical writer, Jan Ruusbroec, was perhaps the most influential and substantial figure among the Flemish mystics. He was greatly influenced by the Be-guines and love mysticism, especially the works of Hadewi-jch. Ruusbroec was originally a parish priest, but at the age of fifty he went with two colleagues to live a secluded life at

---

5. In his *German Sermons*, 69. See Meister Eckhart, *The Essential Sermons, Commentaries, Treatises and Defense* (Mahwah, NJ: Paulist Press, 1981).

6. See Frank Tobin, ed., *Henry Suso: The Exemplar, with Two German Sermons* (Mahwah, NJ: Paulist Press, 1989).

Groenendaal, in the modern-day Netherlands. There they founded a community of Augustinian Canons. One of his major works, *The Spiritual Espousals*, was written before he went to Groenendaal. However, there he wrote a number of other treatises, for example, *The Sparkling Stone*. Like Hadewi-jch, Ruusbroec wrote of our human union with God as a communion of love. His love mysticism is theological rather than simply devotional. Like Julian of Norwich, his writing is notable for its strong emphasis on the image of the Trinity in the human soul. Ruusbroec also strongly criticized any tendency to separate the search for a loving union with God from an obligation to pursue Christian action and ethical behavior.[7]

Finally, the explicit influence of medieval love mysticism extended into the seventeenth century, paradoxically in the writings both of an English Puritan and, later in the century, of a French Catholic woman. Puritanism was a strand of radical Protestantism which flourished in England and later in America, especially in New England. Theologically, Puritanism was Calvinist in tone with an emphasis on spiritual and moral renewal. However, Puritanism's familiar ascetical stance was balanced in some people by a more mystical element. A notable Puritan, Isaac Ambrose, derived spiritual elements in his writings both from medieval Cistercian sermons on the Song of Songs and also from Bridal Mysticism. He explicitly cited these sources.[8] Later in the century, the controversial French woman writer, Madame Guyon, became associated with what Church authorities interpreted as an excessively passive understanding of contemplation and with the notion of total surrender to the initiative of God. However, in her *Commentary on the Canticle*, Guyon focused on the Song of

---

7. See James Wiseman, ed., *John Ruusbroec: The Spiritual Espousals and Other Works* (Mahwah, NJ: Paulist Press, 1985).

8. See Tom Schwanda, *Soul Recreation: The Contemplative-Mystical Piety of Puritanism* (Eugene, OR: Wipf & Stock, 2012).

Songs and followed in the long tradition of love mysticism. Her works on prayer (for example, *A Short and Easy Method of Prayer*) had a wide following and emphasized both affectivity and a kind of objectless mystical contemplation.

SPIRITUAL DESIRE

More broadly, the theme of spiritual longing and desire is present in a number of other Christian mystical writers, such as Julian of Norwich, Teresa of Avila, John of the Cross, as well as the Anglicans George Herbert and Thomas Traherne.

A central theme in the writings of the English woman mystic, Julian of Norwich, is that love is God's very meaning. In what is called her Long Text, Julian declares in chapter 6, "For truly our lover [God] desires the soul to adhere to him with all its power." With God's help, we "persevere in spiritual contemplation, with endless wonder at this high, surpassing, immeasurable love which our Lord in his goodness has for us."[9] In chapter 73, she also affirms that God wants us "in all things to have our contemplation and our delight in love." Also, at the heart of her teaching about prayer, Julian uses the powerful words "longing" and "desire." As early as chapter 5, she exclaims, "God of your goodness give me yourself, for you are enough for me." Because we cannot be completely satisfied in this present life, "therefore it is fitting for us to live always in sweet prayer and in loving longing with our Lord Jesus" (chapter 40). Later in her Fourteenth Revelation, chapters 41–43 develop Julian's teaching on prayer-as-relationship.

9. For a modern translation of Julian's text, see Edmund Colledge and James Walsh, eds., *Julian of Norwich: Showings* (Mahwah, NJ: Paulist Press, 1978). A recent study of Julian's teachings and theology is Philip Sheldrake, *Julian of Norwich: In God's Sight. Her Theology in Context* (Hoboken, NJ: Wiley Blackwell, 2019).

God is the very ground of our longing. Everything that God makes us long for is God's own eternal desire for us.

Moving to the sixteenth century, the reform of the Carmelite Order in Spain and its rich mystical teachings was a striking spiritual movement. The writings of Teresa of Avila and of John of the Cross are among the greatest classics of Western mystical literature. Both Teresa and John were strongly influenced by the Song of Songs and by the medieval mystical tradition of spiritual marriage. It is now widely recognized that both Teresa and John had partly Jewish ancestry, and in her great classic, *The Interior Castle,* Teresa seems to have been influenced by a Jewish mystical text, *The Zohar.* Teresa describes the Christian inner life in terms of a journey through different rooms or mansions of the "castle" of the soul. Finally, this inner journey reaches a climax in rooms five to seven, where there takes place a transforming union with God experienced as a mystical experience of "spiritual marriage." John of the Cross, in his writings on the spiritual journey, such as the *Ascent of Mount Carmel, The Dark Night, The Spiritual Canticle,* and the *Living Flame of Love* emphasizes a process of stripping away our everyday desires that are necessarily less than "everything." These stand in the way of our union with the God who is "all" (*todo* in John's own language). Importantly, in the *Ascent of Mount Carmel,* the "summit" of the spiritual mountain is mystical union described as a spiritual marriage between God and the soul. Finally, in his outstanding poetry, especially *Llama de amor viva* (*The Living Flame of Love*), John talks of the "burning flames" of our mystical love.[10]

---

10. Kieran Kavanaugh and Otilio Rodriguez, eds., *Teresa of Avila: The Interior Castle* (Mahwah, NJ: Paulist Press, 1979), and Kieran Kavanaugh, ed., *John of the Cross: Selected Writings,* Classics of Western Spirituality (Mahwah, NJ: Paulist Press, 1987). For the poetry of John of the Cross, see, Kathleen Jones, ed., *The Poems of St. John of the Cross,* rev. ed. (Tunbridge Wells: Burns & Oates, 2001).

Finally, the seventeenth-century Anglican priests, poets, and spiritual writers, George Herbert and Thomas Traherne, have rich writings on the theme of spiritual desire. The theme of spiritual desire is beautifully portrayed in Herbert's poems.[11] In his poetic collection known as *The Temple*, George Herbert emphasizes that human beings are creatures of desire who struggle to respond to God's own love and desire. In the poem "Discipline" (verse 2) Herbert affirms:

> For my heart's desire
> Unto Thine is bent:
> I aspire
> To a full consent.

God's own being and activity are powerfully expressed in terms of love rather than judgment. In the poem known as "Love (1)," God is described as "Immortal Love." In another poem known as "Love (2)," God's love is described as "Immortal Heat" whose "flame" arouses powerful desires within us. Verse 4 of Herbert's poem "Evensong" concludes with the affirmation that God is nothing but love.

> My God, thou art all love.
> Not one poor minute scapes thy breast
> But brings a favor from above;
> And in this love, more than in bed, I rest.

It appears that George Herbert's desire for God was not a simple matter. Indeed, a notable thread running through his poetry is that his relationship with God was an intense inner spiritual struggle. The most powerful and beautiful expression

11. See Philip Sheldrake, ed., *Heaven in Ordinary: George Herbert and His Writings* (Norwich: Canterbury Press, 2009). Also see John N. Hall, ed., *George Herbert—The Country Parson; The Temple* (Mahwah, NJ: Paulist Press, 1981).

of Herbert's struggles with desire is the final poem of the central section of *The Temple*, entitled "Love (3)." Here, God is named as Love. God welcomes the person at the heart of the poem (doubtless George Herbert) and invites him to join a feast. This is a clear reference to the heavenly banquet but with strong echoes of the service of Holy Communion. Herbert comes across as someone who desperately wants to be worthy before accepting an invitation to the feast. His instinctive desire is to merit God's love. Thus, in the poem Herbert suggests that what is lacking at God's feast is "A guest . . . worthy to be here." This concern underlines a vital spiritual question present throughout Herbert's poetic collection. How is Herbert to surrender himself to God's love? It is only by surrendering that Herbert (an image of all of us) can allow God freely to love him and, indeed, to serve him. Herbert's human desire to be worthy of God seems entirely right. However, on the other hand, this way of desiring focuses on our own ability to live correctly as the key to our relationship with God. Instead, Herbert is gradually led to see that God's own freely expressed desire for us is the key to everything. In this powerful poem, God is shown as the one who loves human beings irrespective of whether they have made themselves worthy or not. The truth is that God desires to give us everything unconditionally. At the end of the poem, Herbert finally surrenders his own desires, including the desire to be worthy of God, and accepts God's desire for him to enter the banquet and to sit down and eat. In that realization and surrender, Herbert finds spiritual freedom.

> Love bade me welcome: yet my soul drew back
>   Guilty of dust and sin.
> But quick-ey'd Love, observing me grow slack
>   From my first entrance in,
> Drew nearer to me, sweetly questioning,
>   If I lack'd anything.
>
> A guest, I answer'd, worthy to be here:
>   Love said, you shall be he.

I the unkind, ungrateful? Ah my dear,
    I cannot look on thee.
Love took my hand, and smiling did reply,
    Who made the eyes but I?

Truth Lord, but I have marr'd them: let my shame
    Go where it doth deserve.
And know you not, says Love, who bore the blame?
    My dear, then I will serve.
You must sit down says Love, and taste my meat:
    So I did sit and eat. ("Love 3")

Later in the seventeenth century, the evocative meditations entitled *Centuries* and the poems by the Anglican priest
Thomas Traherne have a striking mystical edge which is highlighted by the Traherne scholar, the late Denise Inge, in her
introduction to a selection of Traherne's writings, *Happiness
and Holiness: Thomas Traherne and His Writings*.[12] While
Traherne's mystical sensibility frequently relates to a sense of
union with creation, he also had an intense experience of God.
Traherne was led to see that God is a God of desire. Indeed,
Traherne is one of the most beautiful spiritual writers on the
theme of desire—both God's desire and our own. First of all,
there is a poem entitled "Desire."

For giving me desire,
An eager thirst, a burning ardent fire,
A virgin infant flame,
A love with which into the world I came,
An inward hidden heavenly love,
Which in my soul did work and move,
And ever ever me inflame,
With restless longing heavenly avarice,
That never could be satisfied,

---

12. See Denise Inge, *Happiness and Holiness: Thomas Traherne and His
Writings* (Norwich: Canterbury Press, 2008); see also Inge's *Wanting like
a God: Desire and Freedom in Thomas Traherne* (London: SCM Press, 2009).

That did incessantly a Paradise
Unknown suggest, and something undescribed
Discern, and bear me to it; be
Thy name for ever prais'd by me. ("Desire")[13]

Then, in his prose meditations, Traherne asserts:

> You must want like a God that you may be satisfied like
> God. Were you not made in his image[?] . . . His wants
> are as lively as his enjoyments: always present with him.
> For his life is perfect and he feels them both. His wants
> put a lustre upon his enjoyments and make them infinite.
> (Traherne, *Centuries*, 1.44) [14]

"You must want like a God." For Traherne, our human desire
is actually the image within us of a God of desire. Indeed,
for Traherne, God could not be God without desire. This is
because "want is the fountain of all His fullness." Traherne
suggests that "had there been no need He would not have
created the world, nor made us, nor manifested His wisdom
nor exercised His power, nor beautified eternity, nor prepared
the Joys of Heaven" (Traherne, *Centuries*, 1.42).

I will now turn to the other two Abrahamic religions, Judaism and Islam, where the theme of spiritual desire is also
present.

DESIRE IN JUDAISM

Jewish spirituality has a strongly practical-ethical approach,
but there is also an important mystical strand across the centuries. The foundation of Jewish mysticism is everyday belief

13. Thomas Traherne, *Selected Poems and Prose* (London: Penguin Books,
1991).

14. Thomas Traherne, *Centuries* (London: Mowbray, 1975).

and practices. However, Jewish life focuses strongly on explicitly honoring and communicating with a personal God. God is the creator of all things who freely enters into a covenant relationship with humanity (particularly the "chosen" Jewish people). Human beings have a spiritual dimension to their lives (the soul) that is capable of a relationship with God and of communicating with God. The covenant relationship with God is expressed in Jewish ritual practices, as well as in God's gift of the Torah (that is, divine law).

The most famous form of Jewish mysticism is known as Kabbalah. This should not be confused with later esoteric Western movements. Jewish Kabbalah is a set of spiritual teachings that seek to explain the relationship between an eternal, mysterious God and our limited human lives. The source for Kabbalah is an intensive study of and reflection upon the Scriptures. The mystical theology of Kabbalah teaches that the unperceived dimensions of existence are the truly real. The teachings of Kabbalah seek to explain the inner meaning of the Scriptures, of later rabbinical writings, and of everyday Jewish observances such as God's Torah. Importantly, the person who follows the Kabbalah path does not seek a self-focused spiritual journey but is someone who through meticulous study hopes to unlock the deeper mystical dimension of Scripture. There is an intimate connection between common rituals, ethical action, and mystical experience. In that sense, Kabbalah is deeply orthodox.

God has two aspects, according to Kabbalah. One is God's transcendent being, which is necessarily beyond human perception. The other aspect is God's interactive relationship with creation and with humanity. God's creative life force and the unknowable divine essence is channeled through what are called the *sefiroth*—"emanations" of the divine. These are simply different manifestations of the one God. A central Kabbalist doctrine is the relationship between these divine emanations and human ethical behavior. Prayer, allied with ethical and ritual behavior, leads the human spirit on a journey towards the recognition of the true meaning of God's "names." The ultimate state of the mystic is "clinging to God." This comes close to the concept of union in Christian mysticism. However, the final mystical state is not absorption into the divine but an experience of loving intimacy in which God nevertheless remains radically "other."

An important Kabbalah mystical text is *The Zohar* which, as we saw earlier, influenced Teresa of Avila. This is not really a single book but a collection of works in both Hebrew and Aramaic. The texts first appeared in Spain during the Middle Ages when Sephardic Jews were at the forefront not only of a synthesis between Judaism and ancient Greek philosophy (for example the work of Maimonides) but also of the development of a mystical strand in relation to the Pentateuch, the nature of the human soul, and the process of creation. One key to *The Zohar* is the complexity of God, who includes both male and female elements. Also, creation has both visible and hidden aspects, which the mystical unlocks. In *The Zohar*, the practice of prayer goes beyond ritual duty to become a means of reaching intimate union with God.

In the Ashkenasi Judaism of Northern and Eastern Europe, the Kabbalah had some influence. However, a second mystical form emerged, known as Hasidism, during the eighteenth century. While Hasidism is partly influenced by the Kabbalah, it is particularly associated with the teachings of Israel ben Eliezer and, in some ways, is a reaction against an excessive intellectualism among rabbis.

Hasidism is egalitarian in its teachings and emphasizes the value of ordinary Jews and their spiritual lives. Prayer leads to inner happiness rather than just being a ritual duty. Israel ben Eliezer adopted a more devotional approach than the Kabbalah, including fervent recitation of the psalms while concentrating on the inner meaning of each verse. His teachings placed a strong emphasis on a direct love of God present in everyone and everything. This should lead to respect and care for other people. Our daily activities and human relations are potentially the medium for a spiritual, even mystical, interaction with God. In this way, everyday Jews could reach the mystical state of *devekut* or inner "cleaving" to God.

DESIRE IN ISLAM

In Islam, mystical ideas appeared early on, partly in reaction to a growing emphasis on the formalism of rituals and on obedience to divine law. The most famous mystical form of Islam is Sufism, which embraced both the Sunni and Shia communities. Sufism defined itself as simply connecting with Islam's inner core and was believed to originate with Muhammad himself. Firstly, mystical insight is based on constant meditation upon the Qur'an. Second, Sufism implies an imitation of Muhammad's own intense connection to God. Finally, it is said that Sufi teachings were communicated directly by the Prophet to those whom he judged had the right capacity.

Without rejecting normal Islamic practice, Sufism emphasizes a life of love and pure devotion to God and seeks to turn the human heart away from all that is not God. Disciples wish to journey into God's presence and to purify their inner selves. Everyone has a capacity to touch God in ecstatic union (*fana*). According to one version, the Sufi path has four stages: fulfilling the law (repentance), the way (renunciation), spiritual wisdom (trust and patience), and finally, reaching true reality. This echoes classic Christian mystical teaching on the "three ways" of purification, illumination, and union. In Sufi teaching, ecstatic union sometimes involved spiritual annihilation. Thus, when practitioners are purified of material desires and exist in the love of God, they have "annihilated" their individual will and dwell only in and for God. "Annihilation" also involved a submission of the human will to God who provides all that we need in life.

Sufism embraces a range of spiritual practices in the quest for deeper mystical knowledge. The foundation of orthodox Sufism is to be a devoted Muslim who follows the normal laws and practices of Islam. However, Sufism also suggests that the Qur'an has a deeper spiritual meaning. This can only be appreciated through intense spiritual practice, including a rigorous adherence to the practice of prayer five times a day, fasting, and extra practices derived from the life of the Prophet. These sometimes lead to ecstasy, although that is not their purpose.

One spiritual practice strongly commended by some Sufi orders was *dhikr* or meditative concentration on the names for God. This focused the mind and heart on God alone. This practice sometimes involved, together with other people, rhythmically repeating the names out loud, often accompanied by music or dancing. Many Sufis use sets of beads to repeat the traditional ninety-nine names for God drawn from the Qur'an.

Within Sufism there is the varied practice of *muraqaba*, which echoes meditation practices in Christianity. One example is to concentrate all the bodily senses, then to silence all preoccupations that fill the mind, and finally to turn full awareness towards God. The phrase "My God, you are my goal, and your pleasure is what I seek" is recited three times. The heart is then focused on the name of God, remaining in a state of awareness of God's all-encompassing presence. Some Sufi traditions also meditate by linking the repetition of God's name to breathing. There have been suggestions that this Sufi practice may have influenced late medieval Spanish Christian mystics.

According to Sufism, the spiritual seeker needs a teacher or *shaykh*—not only because guidance is critically important but also because this guarantees authentic wisdom through an unbroken line of spiritual teaching going back to the Prophet. Such interpersonal relationships are the key to reaching mystical depths. What stands in the way of spiritual growth is the disordered human ego. Thus, submitting oneself to the guidance of a teacher was an important discipline. This echoes the teachings on obedience to the spiritual father or mother in early Christian desert monasticism.

Three historic Sufi teachers summarize important aspects of the tradition. In chronological order, these are Rabiah al-Basri (c717–801CE), Abu Hamid Mohammad ibn Mohammad al-Ghazali (c1058–1111CE), known in the West as al-Ghazali, and the great poet Jalal ad-Din Mohammad Rumi (1207–1273CE), known in the Western world simply as Rumi.

Rabiah al-Basri was born in what is now southern Iraq. She is remembered as a saint and mystic. She came from a poor family and, after time as a servant, was freed. She went off into the desert and became a solitary, spending long hours in contemplation. She was clear that she wished to remain celibate and to dedicate her life solely to God. Her spiritual reputation attracted many disciples. Although Rabiah left no definite writings, a range of poetry was attributed to her, although much of this is of unknown origin. Equally, many anecdotes were recorded, as were her basic teachings on love of God. God should be loved simply for God's own sake and not out of duty.

Al-Ghazali was of Persian origin and became a major thinker, expert on Islamic law, and ultimately a mystic. Initially, he focused on Islamic philosophy, but a spiritual crisis in midlife led to a major change of direction. He adopted an ascetic, wandering lifestyle. After visiting Mecca and spending some ten years in Syria and Palestine, he returned to Persia, where he lived a life of simplicity and seclusion, writing, meditating, and teaching. He also founded a *khanqah*, or center for study, sometimes loosely referred to as a "Sufi monastery." Such centers were designed as gathering places for spiritual retreat and sometimes as the residence for a *shaykh*, as well as for Sufis who wished to lead lives of spiritual practice in quiet solitude. Overall, al-Ghazali coordinated orthodox Islam with a systematic approach to Sufism and wrote more than seventy books. One of his most influential works was a spiritual autobiography written towards the end of his life. In particular, al-Ghazali discussed his intellectual crisis and experience of being illuminated by

God. In the end, he found value only in the mystical way associated with Sufism. Al-Ghazali was a significant influence on the medieval Christian thinker Thomas Aquinas.

Sufism also has a literary tradition that amplifies the teachings of the Qur'an through devotional poetry focused on love of God. The famous Persian mystic poet Rumi believed in the transformative power of words in themselves. As Rumi commented, the words evoked "the scent of their Beloved and their Quest." Rumi was a theologian, jurist, and Sufi mystic, but he is best known as an important poet who has been translated into numerous languages. Similar to al-Ghazali, in midlife, after some years as a jurist and teacher, Rumi underwent a profound spiritual change and became an ascetic. He composed a collection of lyric poems as well as other writings. Rumi's *Spiritual Couplets* are considered by many to be one of the greatest works of mystical poetry in both Sufism and more generally. Additionally, Rumi composed a further major collection known as the *Great Work*. While Rumi taught a spirituality of divine love that is universally attractive, he remained an orthodox Muslim.

> My soul is mingled with Thee, dissolved in Thee,
> A soul to cherish as it has Thy perfume!
>
> Each drop of blood of mine
> Is saying to Thy dust,
> "I am the colour of Your love,
> Companion of Your affection.
>
> In this house of clay, my heart is desolate
> Without Thee!
> O Beloved, come into this house
> Or else I'll be gone!" ("My Soul")[15]

---

15. On Sufi mysticism, see Annemarie Schimmel, *Mystical Dimensions of Islam* (Chapel Hill: University of North Carolina Press, 1983). For a selection of Rumi's poetry, see Mahmood Jamal, ed., *Islamic Mystical Poetry: Sufi Verse from the Early Mystics to Rumi* (London: Penguin Books, 2009).

Epilogue: Etty Hillesum

I would like to end with a few reflections on a more controversial example of intense desire and spiritual passion: the twentieth-century Dutch writer Etty Hillesum, who came from a secular Jewish family and died in Auschwitz at twenty-nine years old in 1943. Over time, Etty entered into an unconventional but deep spiritual journey expressed in her diaries and letters. Her restless desire and intense spiritual passion, while detached from institutional religion, gave a profoundly mystical tone to her writings as she encountered what she referred to as "the God within."

Etty's story is accessible through her diaries (1941–42).[16] There are also her 1942–43 letters from the Nazi transit camp at Westerbork.

> Our desire must be like a slow and stately ship, sailing across endless oceans, never in search of safe anchorage. (*An Interrupted Life*, 92).

"Never in search of safe anchorage" perfectly summarizes Etty's fearless and never-ending search for inner truth (her "destiny," as she called it) and for moral beauty. She sought to be faithful to love and to her belief in humanity in the face of appalling Nazi brutality. Eventually, her restless desire led Etty to an intense religious sensibility that gives her diaries a profoundly mystical tone. Two things stand out. First, Etty's passionate approach to life was thoroughly embodied in her sexuality. However, beyond her tendency to become impulsively involved with men, she learned how to channel desire into a deeper blend of tender commitment and personal

---

16. Quotations are from Etty Hillesum, *An Interrupted Life* (New York: Washington Square Press, 1985). For the complete diaries and letters, see Klaas A. D. Smelik, ed., *Etty: The Letters and Diaries of Etty Hillesum 1941–1943* (Grand Rapids, MI: Eerdmans, 2002).

freedom. The intensity of Etty's growing mystical awareness led her into active engagement with the surrounding world, finally expressed by voluntarily working for fellow Jews imprisoned at Westerbork and then sharing their terrible fate.

Etty's diary records a painful process of discernment and choice—increasingly from within her deepest self. In this growing self-awareness, Etty also encountered God with an intensity that was arguably mystical.

> I sometimes actually drop to my knees beside my bed, even on a cold winter night. And I listen in to myself, allow myself to be led, not by anything on the outside, but by what wells up from within. (*An Interrupted Life*, 81)

Etty Hillesum talked of her mysterious inner regulator.

> I still believe I have an inner regulator, which warns me every time I take the wrong path by bringing on a "depression." If only I remain honest and open with myself and determined enough to become what I must be and to do what my conscience commands, then everything will turn out all right. (*An Interrupted Life*, 203)

Etty was led from her many desires to her center or essential self. Here, where she was in contact with her deepest desire, she found that she was essentially attuned to God.

> There is a really deep well inside me. And in it dwells God. Sometimes I am there too. But more often stones and grit block the well, and God is buried beneath. Then He must be dug out again. (*An Interrupted Life*, 44)

CHAPTER FOUR

KNOWING AND UNKNOWING

The theme of "knowing" and "unknowing" is another important aspect of mysticism, not least in the Christian tradition. In one sense, mysticism leads to a kind of transfiguration of human knowledge and to a new level of enlightenment regarding God and the transcendent.

One striking example is the Eastern Christian tradition of "hesychasm" (from the Greek word *hēsychia*—quietness or stillness,). From the time of the early desert fathers and mothers up to the Middle Ages, the concept of "hesychasm" was regularly identified with monastic withdrawal and a life of contemplation. However, the term gradually came to be understood as a state of stillness arrived at through intense spiritual practice where we are freed from mental images and from desire. This is a prelude to an intimate encounter with God. By the late thirteenth century CE, under the influence of such figures as Gregory Palamas (1296–1359), "hesychasm" became a distinctive spiritual tradition. The result was partly a growing emphasis on what is nowadays known as the spiritual practice of the "Jesus Prayer" (or "Prayer of the Name"). Gregory Palamas outlined a way of knowing that transcends human reason, including thoughts and images. The practice known as the Jesus Prayer supports the deepening of an inner spiritual awareness of the presence of God's Spirit. This deep awareness has the capacity to evoke a luminous, even mystical, vision of the transcendent.[1]

However, in relation to what Christianity believes to be ultimately the unknowable quality of God, there is necessarily a permanent tension between knowing and unknowing. To what extent can we be said to possess some "knowledge" of God or of the Absolute? To quote the words of the anonymous fourteenth-century English mystical text, *The Cloud of Unknowing*, "How am I to think of God and what is he? And to this I can only answer 'I do not know.'" During the same period, there was also the enigmatic theological language of the popular Rhineland mystic Meister Eckhart, who talked about the need for us to deny the ways we seek to define God in order to touch the divine "ground"—what we may think of as "the God beyond God." Eckhart also loved to say that "If I have spoken of it [God], I have not spoken, for it [God] is ineffable"!

In terms of the other Abrahamic religions, the Jewish Kabbalah text, *The Zohar* (which may have influenced Teresa of Avila), talked about reaching a deeper mystical knowledge of the Torah, God's law revealed in the books of the Pentateuch. In Islam, the Sufism of Al-Ghazali also touched upon the theme of a deeper knowing in relation to Allah and to the Koran. Hindu and Buddhist mysticism also touch upon issues of knowing and unknowing. Finally, the quest for a hidden knowledge of reality—or superior illumination—is also a characteristic of esoteric movements such as Theosophy and Anthroposophy.

---

1. On the Eastern spiritual tradition, see, e.g., John McGuckin, *Standing in God's Holy Fire: The Byzantine Tradition* (London: Darton, Longman & Todd, 2001); John Chryssavgis, *Light through Darkness: The Orthodox Tradition* (London: Darton, Longman & Todd, 2004); Colm Luibheid, ed., *John Climacus: The Ladder of Divine Ascent*, Classics of Western Spirituality (Mahwah, NJ: Paulist Press, 1982); John Meyendorff, ed., *Gregory Palamas—The Triads*, Classics of Western Spirituality (Mahwah, NJ: Paulist Press, 1983).

CHRISTIAN MYSTICISM AND
A THEOLOGY OF UNKNOWING

As already noted, one of the most fundamental aspects of the Christian approach to God is that all human relationships with God embrace a paradox of knowing and not knowing. This tension between some degree of knowledge and the limitations of human knowing in relation to God is particularly powerful in Christian mystical writings.

The history of Christianity is often presented purely in terms of a search for doctrinal precision and certainty. However, Christianity has always affirmed that God is ultimately beyond our capacity to know and explain in any definitive sense. A particularly striking image of this limitation appears in the New Testament book of Acts. This is the story of the apostle Peter's vision before his visit to Cornelius and his family as described in chapter ten. As an orthodox Jew, Peter "knew" what God had mandated in terms of dietary laws. However, in his vision at Caesarea, Peter was challenged to eat what classic Jewish dietary laws had declared to be unclean. Understandably, Peter questioned this. However, he heard a voice that said, "What God has made clean, you must not call profane." While visiting Cornelius, an "unclean" Gentile, Peter was led to make an important connection. He came to realize that with God there are no favorites. God is as much the God of the supposedly unclean Gentiles as of the chosen Jewish people. According to this story, God profoundly challenged Peter's assumptions about where God was to be found, how God acts, and how God is to be "known." This challenge to conventional ways of knowing God is forcefully underlined by the narrative that Cornelius and his family received God's Holy Spirit even though they were not baptized (Acts 10:44-48). Basically, the story proclaims that God's Spirit does not always work simply within conventional human boundaries but, on the contrary, "blows where it wills." It is only by accepting this that we allow ourselves to be led by God in the direction of the fullness of truth. The Christian mystical tradition and its associated writings is a story of how Christianity throughout history has struggled with a profound discomfort at the disruptive side of God. Ultimately, God pushes us beyond the comfortable and conventional boundaries of religious doctrines. This forces us to come to terms with God's unpredictable nature and God's way of leading us ever onwards.

As a result, Christian attempts throughout history to talk about God have struggled with the need to find a balance between images of God and recognizing that God's reality is ultimately beyond all human images. The words "cataphatic" (positive) and "apophatic" (negative) have often been used to describe two dimensions of our attempts to talk about God. The cataphatic dimension emphasizes the role of images and of human knowing. This positive theology is based on a Christian understanding that material creation and human life somehow reflect God's nature. Therefore, they are contexts for God's self-revelation. However, by way of contrast, the apophatic dimension of our ways of talking about God emphasizes the radical limitation of any human imagery. It therefore underlines the need for us to move beyond images of God to a way of not knowing—silence and darkness. Only by balancing our imaging of God with the "way of denial" may we tentatively touch a God who is ultimately beyond everything that we can conceive or control.

EARLY CHRISTIAN THOUGHT

Much early Christian theology was apophatic in its mystical dimension. For example, during the late fourth century, a theologian in Constantinople, Evagrius Ponticus (died 399), became a monk in Egypt. His mystical writing speaks of God mainly in the language of negations or denial. It talks of what God is *not* rather than what humans wish to assert about the nature of God. Evagrius used a threefold model of the spiritual journey. This begins with a stage of overcoming our passions, then progresses to a second stage of contemplating creation, and finally reaches its climax with the stage of a mystical union with God-as-Trinity. Evagrius combined speculative Neoplatonic philosophy with desert monastic spiritual practice. This led him to produce teachings on imageless contemplation that had a longstanding influence on Eastern Christian spirituality.[2]

One of the most important spiritual theologians in the patristic period was Gregory of Nyssa (c335–c395), who was one of the so-called Cappadocian Fathers. He is perhaps best remembered through his text of mystical theology, *The Life of Moses*. Like Evagrius, Gregory described the spiritual journey in terms of stages. He also used the image of ascent. However, for Gregory, this journey was towards deep darkness rather than toward greater light. As his narrative framework, Gregory employed the story of Moses in the book of Exodus. Gregory used the metaphor of Moses' ascent of Mount Sinai. Moses entered into ever deeper clouds of darkness as he experienced a challenging encounter with God. Basically, Gregory of Nyssa has an apophatic understanding of the "summit" of the contemplative journey. In this deep cloud of darkness, God may be experienced but is never finally known. For Gregory, the human spiritual journey is a never-ending movement towards perfection in which we never conclusively arrive. Gregory's teachings on the mystical journey had a considerable influence on mystical teaching in both Eastern and Western Christianity.[3]

Pseudo-Dionysius

Turning now to pseudo-Dionysius, this second important writer on mystical theology in early Christian thought was an anonymous monk in Syria who wrote around the year 500

2. See, e.g., John E. Bamberger, ed., *Evagrius Ponticus: The Praktikos; Chapters on Prayer* (Collegeville, MN: Cistercian Publications, 1970).

3. See, e.g., Abraham J. Malherbe, ed., *Gregory of Nyssa: The Life of Moses*, Classics of Western Spirituality (Mahwah, NJ: Paulist Press, 1978).

CE. He was perhaps the single greatest influence on the development of a tradition of Christian mysticism. The monk wrote under the pseudonym of Dionysius, which was the name of Paul's convert described in the book of Acts, chapter 17. Pseudo-Dionysius is best known in the West for his apophatic mystical spirituality, developed in his shortest work, *Mystical Theology*. This was translated from Greek into Latin in the ninth century of the Common Era by the Irish theologian John Scotus Eriugena and thus became accessible to Western Christians. *Mystical Theology*, like Gregory of Nyssa, stressed divine darkness. God is ultimately incomprehensible and beyond all definitions.

Paradoxically, God is "known" by negating all the images for God that we conventionally use. However, merely to stress Dionysius's "negative" theology in isolation would be misleading. Not only did another treatise, *The Divine Names*, deal with God as revealed in the many names used in the Scriptures, but the whole of Dionysius's spiritual theology is centered on the Christian liturgy. In *The Ecclesiastical Hierarchy*, the liturgy is portrayed as drawing all the baptized believers, along with all created reality, into the dynamic of God's self-revelation. According to pseudo-Dionysius, the Christian liturgy not only provides a rich symbolism of the divine but is also an earthly manifestation of the hierarchies that proceed in ordered fashion from God. It would be more accurate to say that pseudo-Dionysius's mystical theology emphasizes that God may be encountered both in human affirmation and in a necessary process of negation or denial.

In other words, in pseudo-Dionysius's approach to God, knowing and unknowing are mutually related features rather than mutually exclusive. The whole of creation is brought into being by God to show forth divine glory. The cosmos is to be viewed positively as the self-revelation of God's goodness. "Good" is, therefore, the first affirmation (or image) of God discussed by pseudo-Dionysius. Again, in pseudo-Dionysius's theology, God-as-Trinity is first described in terms of distinctions between the divine "persons," whereby we can know something of God. However, underlying these distinctions, or contained within them, is a unity or synthesis that we cannot ultimately comprehend. Therefore, the Christian theology of God-as-Trinity is a way of knowing because it seeks to affirm something essential about God. However, at the same time, it is a way of unknowing because the affirmations we make immediately push us beyond what we can fully grasp. Paradoxically, the doctrine of the Trinity may be said to reveal God and yet reveals God as beyond human definitions. Through our relationship with God as revealed in creation, and even in our affirmations, we come to appreciate that God is never our possession or an object of human reason and knowledge. Ultimately, God is beyond both human "knowing" and "unknowing."[4]

MEISTER ECKHART

Another key figure in exploring the themes of knowing and unknowing in Christian mysticism is the fourteenth-century writer Meister Eckhart (c1260–c1328), a Rhineland Dominican theologian and preacher.[5] Eckhart is known only by his academic title of "Meister" or Master. He studied at Cologne and Paris and may have been taught by another famous Dominican, Albert the Great, from whom he gained a taste for the Neoplatonic mysticism of pseudo-Dionysius. This combined with the

4. Colm Luibheid and Paul Rorem, eds., *Pseudo-Dionysius: The Complete Works*, Classics of Western Spirituality (Mahwah, NJ: Paulist Press, 1987).

5. Bernard McGinn and Edmund Colledge, eds., *Meister Eckhart: The Essential Sermons, Commentaries, Treatises, and Defense* (Mahwah, NJ: Paulist Press, 1985); and Bernard McGinn and Frank Tobin, eds., *Meister Eckhart: Teacher and Preacher* (Mahwah, NJ: Paulist Press, 1987). See also Bernard McGinn, *The Mystical Thought of Meister Eckhart* (New York: Crossroad Publishing, 2001).

philosophy of Aristotle as promoted by yet another Dominican, Thomas Aquinas. Eckhart is the object of contemporary
fascination even outside Christianity because of his paradoxical
religious language. On the one hand, he asserted that there is
an absolute abyss separating us from a transcendent mysterious
God. This led Meister Eckhart to speak of a necessary denial
of our concepts of "God" in our quest to reach out towards
a transcendent divine "ground." This may be thought of as
the "God beyond God." However, at the same time Eckhart
also made daring assertions about a mystical identity between
humans and God. He is at his most radically paradoxical in his
vernacular German sermons. Metaphors are used in contradic-
tory ways to reveal deeper meanings. His obscure language led
to suspicions of heresy and the condemnation of some of his
teaching. This is now widely thought to be based on a degree
of misunderstanding.

Overall, the mystical dimension of Christianity questions
the adequacy of all conventional language about God. In line
with this, Meister Eckhart loved to paraphrase Augustine on
speaking about God: "If I have spoken of it, I have not spoken,
for it is ineffable."[6]

THE CLOUD OF UNKNOWING

As another important example, I will now turn to the great
flourishing of mysticism in fourteenth-century England. A case
can be made that the greatest flowering of new spiritual movements, including mystical writings, tends to take place during periods of major social, political, and religious upheaval.
These movements respond to the challenges of their times.
Adversity, anxiety, and uncertainty, plus a decline in people's
overall trust in traditional political and religious systems, often

6. For Meister Eckhart, see, e.g., Sermon 9, German Sermons, in McGinn
and Tobin, eds., *Meister Eckhart: Teacher and Preacher*, 255–61.

provoke the search for a more intense personal engagement with God or the sacred.

Fourteenth-century England (and wider Europe) is sometimes referred to as an "age of adversity" with striking parallels to our own times. The period was characterized by great human suffering through plagues, war, social breakdown, political unrest, and a major schism in the Western Church.[7] This was the painful context for the five people we call "the English mystics." Between them they span the fourteenth century plus the first half of the fifteenth century. Apart from the lay hermit and writer Richard Rolle, the lawyer and theologian Walter Hilton, plus the highly eccentric Margery Kempe, originally married but later a wandering pilgrim in Europe and the Holy Land who dictated her spiritual insights to a sympathetic scribe, there were the two mystical writers with the largest contemporary readership, Julian of Norwich, with her *Revelations of Divine Love*, and the anonymous writer of *The Cloud of Unknowing*.

In the context of this chapter, *The Cloud of Unknowing* is another mystical text that outlines the tension between knowing and unknowing in our relationship with God. The book has become extraordinarily popular in recent decades, including with people who identify themselves as "spiritual" rather than conventionally religious.[8]

The anonymous author of *The Cloud* was probably a Carthusian monk, initially writing his text of spiritual guidance for a younger monk. That said, the author clearly expects the book to be more widely read. First, it is written in vernacular English

7. For an overview, see Joan M. Nuth, *God's Lovers in an Age of Anxiety: The Medieval English Mystics* (London: Darton, Longman & Todd, 2001), chapter 1.

8. Unless noted otherwise, subsequent quotations from *The Cloud of Unknowing* are taken from the Penguin Classics edition. See A. C. Spearing, ed., *The Cloud of Unknowing and Other Works* (London: Penguin Books, 2001).

rather than in Latin. In addition, the opening prologue immediately lists the kinds of people who should not read the book. "I do not desire that this book should be seen by worldly chatterers, public self-praisers or fault-finders, newsmongers, gossips or scandal-mongers or detractors of any kind" (12). However, the author does not suggest that his writings are only for monks or not for laypeople. Rather, the author lays out a range of attitudes that get in the way of spiritual wisdom. Who is the advice intended for? The prologue of the text offers some initial ideas. First, it is for the benefit of people who have a commitment to being "perfect follower[s] of Christ." Interestingly, they have also prepared for the way of contemplation by "virtuous active living" (11). Sometimes the book suggests that its spiritual teaching is for those who have left the active life behind, but in the prologue, it speaks of those who are in the active life "externally" but are inwardly stirred by God to be strongly inclined towards what he calls the "highest contemplation" (12).

We will come to what he means by "highest contemplation" in a moment, but the author is clear that there are no shortcuts. We should not prematurely try to adopt contemplative practice before we are ready for a truly contemplative attitude. Indeed, our values and attitudes count for far more than specific spiritual *practices*. So, in chapter 35, the author talks about being prepared by a regular practice of the monastic style of scriptural meditation known as *lectio divina*: "All the same, intermediate activities do exist in which an apprentice in contemplation ought to be occupied, and they are these: Lection, Meditation, and Orison. For your better understanding these may be called Reading, Thinking, and Praying" (58). In several chapters, for example, chapters 15, 16, 28, 31, 35, and 75, the author also mentions that as Christians we prepare for the highest contemplation through taking part in the Church's liturgical and sacramental life.

In terms of the focus of this chapter, *The Cloud* refers to what is known as apophatic contemplation—the so-called negative way. In summary, this is the quest to reach union with the Divine through discernment of what God is *not* rather than by describing what God *is*. In terms of prayer, this emphasizes coming to God in silence and stillness rather than with many words, and through love rather than by our intellect. This "immediacy of presence" to God cannot be constructed by us. Rather, it is a gift based on God's invitation to us. In other words, this immediacy of presence concerns a deeply embedded attitude of heart and a wholehearted loving commitment "to be" with the One who simply "is."

As the author of *The Cloud* suggests, we reach a "cloud of unknowing." That is, there develops an absence of all intellectual or rational activity. We end up by simply resting contentedly in darkness.

> But now you ask me, "How am I to think of God himself, and what is he?" And to this I can only answer "I do not know." For with your question you have brought me into that very darkness and that very cloud of unknowing that I want you to be in yourself. . . . And so I wish to give up everything that I can think and choose as my love the one thing I cannot think. For he [God] can well be loved but he cannot be thought. . . . In the work of contemplation it [i.e., thought] must be . . . covered with a cloud of forgetting. And you must step above it . . . with a devout and delightful stirring of love and struggle to pierce that darkness above you; and beat on that thick cloud of unknowing with a sharp dart of longing love and do not give up whatever happens. (chapter 6).

Is any spiritual practice involved? To some extent it is, as chapter 7 of *The Cloud* makes clear. "Therefore, whenever you resolve to undertake this work of contemplation, and feel that by grace you are called by God, lift up your heart to God with a humble stirring of love" (29). There is more. "If you want to have this intention wrapped and enfolded in one word . . . take only a short word of one syllable. . . . A word of this kind is the word GOD or the word LOVE. Choose whichever you wish or another if you please . . . and fasten this word to your heart so that it never parts from it whatever happens" (29). The author of *The Cloud* does not say precisely what we are to do with this word. Are we to recite it, or are we to think of it? However, broadly, it is enough to hold the chosen word as the sole focus in what he refers to as "the mind's eye."

As the author of *The Cloud* suggests, at its heart the way of "unknowing" does not imply an absence of meaning. Rather, it is simply a process of leaving behind our quest for intellectual certainty in favor of simply resting in God's love.

> Now all rational creatures, angels and men alike, have in them, each one individually, one chief working power which is called a knowing power, and another chief working power called a loving power; and of these two powers, God, who is the maker of them, is always incomprehensible to the first, the knowing power. But to the second, which is the loving power, he is entirely comprehensible. . . .

> No man can think of God himself. Therefore, It is my wish to leave everything that I can think of and choose for my love the thing I cannot think. Because [God] can certainly be loved but not thought. (*The Cloud of Unknowing*, chapters IV and VI)[9]

Even our pious thoughts, as well as our theological musings, about the nature of God need to be pushed down below what the author of *The Cloud* calls "the cloud of forgetting" when it comes to our ultimate contemplative presence to God (see chapter 8, p. 32). Sometimes readers have accused the author of being anti-intellectual or of not being concerned enough with theological orthodoxy. However, the text is actually theologically sophisticated, and the author is loyal to the church. It

---

9. See the modern edition by James Walsh, *The Cloud of Unknowing* (Mahwah, NJ: Paulist Press, 1981), chapters IV and VI.

is just that in the contemplative process, whatever is less than God's own challenging presence should not preoccupy us. To be clear, according to the author, "the cloud of forgetting" lies below our spiritual space and separates us from all our previous preoccupations. The "cloud of unknowing" lies above us and separates us from an ultimately mysterious God. As chapter 6 reminds us, "by love God can be grasped and held but by thought neither grasped nor held" (28). The essence of the way of higher contemplation is therefore a simple presence to God or an immediate encounter. Thus, at the beginning of chapter 3, the author teaches: "Lift up your heart towards God with a humble stirring of love; and think of himself not of any good to be gained from him." Also, in the last paragraph of chapter 3, he affirms:

> Do not give up but labor at it until you feel desire. For the first time you do it, you will find only darkness and as it were a cloud of unknowing. . . . And so prepare to remain in this darkness as long as you can, always begging for him you love; for if you are ever to feel or see him, so far as it is possible in this life, it must always be in this cloud and this darkness. (22)

Finally, what are the results of this contemplative path? They may include some kind of "consolation"—that is, an abundance of devotion or the sense of sweetness and pleasure. However, this is not necessary, and we must not become dependent on such things (see the first paragraph of chapters 50 and 74). What is more important is how this contemplative path transforms our lives—especially deepening certain key virtues. According to *The Cloud*, an important virtue is that of humility (chapter 2, first paragraph, pp. 20–21). This is the growing capacity to model oneself on the humility of Jesus Christ. There is more detail on the virtue of humility in chapter 13 (pp. 36–37). In addition, the heights of contemplation must not be separated from the virtues of charity and of service of other people.

A perfect worker in contemplation has no regard to any
specific person for his own sake, whether kin or stranger,
friend or foe, for all alike seem kin to him and none seems
a stranger. All seem his friends and none his enemies so that
for him all those who torment him and cause him distress
on earth are his particular friends, and he feels moved to
desire as much good for them as he would for the closest
friend he has. (chapter 24, p. 49, final paragraph)

THE HIDDEN FACE OF GOD

In summary, in Christian mysticism, seeking God through
images prevents us from losing touch with God's movement
towards us in creation, in our own lives, and in God's self-
revelation in the person of Jesus Christ. On the other hand, we
cannot reduce God to human imagery. Within the Christian
tradition, God has always received many names, while remaining beyond every name. Indeed, the apparently endless process
of "naming" of God implicitly draws us back into the mysterious divine depths that are beyond the limitations of naming,
of reason, and of human experience. Difficult though it may
sound, the Christian tradition suggests that we must hold in
creative tension the process of imaging God and the process
of denial that any image is really God. For some people, apophatic or negative theology is ultimately normative. In the
words of the important British theologian Rowan Williams,
"Apophasis is 'not a branch of theology,' but an attitude which
should undergird *all* theological discourse, and lead it towards
the silence of contemplation and communion."[10]

It is interesting that a number of contemporary analyses
of the implications for Christian spirituality of postmodern

---

10. See Rowan Williams, "The Via Negativa and The Foundations of
Theology: An Introduction to the Thought of V. N. Lossky," in *New Studies
in Theology*, vol. 1, ed. Stephen Sykes and Derek Holmes (London: Duckworth,
1980), 96. Italics are in the original.

approaches to experience reflect these central paradoxes in the doctrine of God. We may now realize once again that the world is ultimately beyond the capacity of the human mind to fully grasp. However, this should not be a recipe for despair. Rather, it opens up the possibility of a return to a sense of wonder at the heart of our theology and spirituality.

One recent analysis of spirituality in the contemporary post-modern context speaks of a number of crucial needs that relate directly to the doctrine of God. Spirituality must be strongly incarnational and engaged with the ordinariness of material reality. It should emphasize the existential nature of God's relationship to us. It should encourage a radical belief in the unconditional love of God behind all reality, including "the monstrosities of history." Finally, it should speak of the cross of Christ as the suffering of God within human suffering. Some postmodernist writing (for example, the work of Jacques Derrida) has been described as a form of apophatic or "negative" theology.[11] Whether or not this view is appropriate, contemporary approaches to mysticism need to reflect upon the tradition of God's "hiddenness" in the context of a contemporary "absence of God" in the lives of many Western people.

A significant twentieth-century religious poet, the Welsh Anglican priest R. S. Thomas, beautifully captures a kind of postmodern "dark night of the soul." Faith is stripped to its bare essentials and God's presence is paradoxically experienced only in absence.

> Why no! I never thought other than
> That God is that great absence
> In our lives, the empty silence
> Within, the place where we go

---

11. Rowan Williams, "Hegel and the Gods of Postmodernity," in *Shadow of Spirit: Postmodernism and Religion*, ed. Philippa Berry and Andrew Wernick (London: Routledge, 1992), 73–80.

Seeking, not in hope to
Arrive or find . . . [12]

Overall, the hidden face of God plays a particularly strong role in the Christian tradition of mysticism. The believer is brought to the frontiers of human language and of conceptual thinking and arrives at the edge of mystery—a Mystery which is, nevertheless, intensely present. It is not surprising that the great French Jesuit intellectual, Michel de Certeau, draws parallels between postmodern culture and the mystical tradition. Both the mystic and the postmodern person live in a kind of movement of perpetual departure. They are wanderers and pilgrims who, in the words of de Certeau, are lost in "the totality of the immense." Each of them "with the certainty of what is lacking, knows of every place and object that it is *not that*, one cannot stay *there* nor be content with *that*."[13]

As de Certeau underlined, the culture of what is known as "modernity" placed a powerful emphasis on intelligibility, not least in our language about God. Because of this, those people whose lives affirm the essential otherness of a mysterious God were seen by de Certeau as outsiders to the "modern" project.[14] Echoing de Certeau, the American theologian David Tracy suggests that hope lies particularly in the challenge to traditional power and privilege offered by the "otherness" present in marginal groups. Tracy points particularly to the mystics and the mad.[15] As I have already suggested in chapter 2, perhaps this is why de Certeau was fascinated throughout his writings by the seventeenth-century Jesuit mystic Jean-Joseph Surin

---

12. From the poem "Via Negativa," in R. S. Thomas, *Later Poems* (London: Macmillan, 1983).

13. Michel de Certeau, *The Mystic Fable*, vol. 1, ET (Chicago: University of Chicago Press, 1992), 299. The emphases are the author's.

14. De Certeau, *Mystic Fable*, especially the introduction, 1–26.

15. David Tracy, *On Naming the Present: God, Hermeneutics, and the Church* (Maryknoll, NY: Orbis Books, 1994), 3–6.

(whom he called "my guardian"). For many years Surin was also profoundly disturbed psychologically and consequently was oppressed and became isolated from the mainstream.[16]

MYSTICISM IN WORLD RELIGIONS

Mysticism in the three strongly scriptural Abrahamic religions—Judaism, Christianity, and Islam—is as much concerned with religious language as it is with inner experience. In that context, mysticism can be understood as a quest to reach out to a God who is ultimately beyond our ability to capture in human language. The mystical traditions of the three Abrahamic religions radically question the adequacy of all the words we conventionally seek to use about God. Can we actually define or ultimately name God? The mystical traditions of Judaism, Christianity, and Islam all answer the question with a clear no. Yet, all three religions maintain a vital tension between using images of God or names for God, as outlined in their Scriptures, and a way of "unknowing" or "denial."

Turning to Jewish mysticism, at its heart are fundamental teachings about God and how God relates to human existence. Judaism believes in a single God who is wholly other and ultimately mysterious. However, this God is also described as "creator"—the source of everything that exists and the power that continues to maintain everything in existence. In the light of the Jewish Scriptures, embracing both the foundational vision of God in the book of Genesis and historical narratives of God's relationship with the Jewish people, there is also a redemptive side to God. This acts as an ongoing symbol of human hope in the midst of the limitations and pain of our

16. See *Mystic Fable*, passim but especially chapter 7, "The Enlightened Illiterate." De Certeau also edited the work of Surin: *Jean-Joseph Surin: Correspondence* (Paris: Desclée, 1963) and *Jean-Joseph Surin: Guide Spirituel pour La Perfection* (Paris: Desclée, 1963).

everyday lives. There is also a belief in the eventual arrival of God's Messiah, who will save humanity.

In Judaism, while God is wholly "other" and transcendent, God nevertheless seeks to communicate with us. This is expressed in the Jewish tradition of prophecy that began with Moses and is expressed in a number of important books in the Jewish Scriptures (known by Christians as the Old Testament). The vision of God expressed by the Torah, or Jewish law, is of one who seeks to be revealed to the Jewish people. In other words, Judaism, like Christianity and Islam, is a religion of God's self-revelation. In terms of "knowing" God, there have always been debates in Judaism (as in the other Abrahamic religions) between those who see the texts of the Hebrew Scriptures as the literal, dictated "word of God" and those who believe that God's self-communication is mediated through human words which then need interpretation.

In Judaism, there are two explicit mystical strands—Hasidism and Kabbalah. The latter is the best-known form of Jewish mysticism. This must not be confused with later esoteric Western forms which embrace astrology and magic. Jewish Kabbalah offers teachings that seek to explain how an eternal, mysterious God relates to finite human lives. The sources for the mystical tradition of Kabbalah are basically the result of intensive reflection upon the Scriptures rather than any other independent spiritual practices. The mystical teachings of Kabbalah suggest that the unperceived, spiritual dimensions of existence are in fact the truly "real." The teachings of Kabbalah seek to lead practitioners to unlock the deeper mystical meaning of the Scriptures as well as of later rabbinical teachings and even the mystical potential of everyday Jewish practice. Thus, Kabbalah is founded on the Torah, Jewish law expressed in the Pentateuch, plus the observance of God's commandments (*mitzvot*). The latter are the most perfect expression of God's will and of how humanity may relate to God.

God is central to Kabbalism and is understood to have two aspects. One is the transcendent side, which is necessarily

beyond human definition. The other aspect of God is immanent. That is, God is revealed in and through an interactive
relationship with the world and with humanity. Within this
immanent aspect of God is the concept of *sefiroth* or *sephirot*. These are emanations or manifestations of the One God,
which channel the divine life force to the created world and
reveal the ultimately unknowable divine essence. There are
ten rungs of *sefiroth*. Prayer, along with an ethical life and
ritual behavior, leads believers on a journey ever upward to
recognize the true meaning of God's "names." According to
Kabbalah, the ultimate state of the mystic is one of "clinging
to God." This is an equivalent of the concept of "union" with
God in Christian mystical literature. However, like "union,"
the image of "clinging" still leaves a clear distinction between
God and human beings. The ultimate mystical state is an experience of loving intimacy in which the eternal God nevertheless remains radically other, mysterious, and unknowable.
The text *The Zohar*, which was mentioned in the last chapter,
discussed reaching a deeper mystical knowledge of the law of
God, the Torah, as revealed in the books of the Pentateuch.[17]

In terms of Islam, the great mystical tradition of Sufism
crosses the boundaries between the two main religious group-
ings known as the Sunni and the Shia. In Islam, certain beliefs
are prescriptive. In broad terms, the most fundamental are that
God is One and that the purpose of human life is to be obedi-
ent to God. While the notion of obedience to God's laws has
great prominence, some elements within Islam also promote
an image of God as one who loves humanity and of the human
duty to love God in return. Adherents also believe that Islam
is the definitive religious faith that completes and corrects the

17. For an authoritative study of Jewish mysticism and spirituality, see
the essays by different authors in the two volumes of *Jewish Spirituality*, ed.
Arthur Green (New York: Crossroad, 1987). For an overview summary of
Jewish mysticism, see Philip Sheldrake, *Spirituality: A Guide for the Perplexed*
(London: Bloomsbury, 2014), chapter 5.

tradition of divine revelation that embraces the earlier prophets, Abraham, Moses, and Jesus. The scriptural text of Islam, the Qur'an (known as the Koran in English), is understood to be the final and complete revelation of God. Islam is fiercely monotheistic. In chapter, or *sura*, 112 of the Qur'an, God is the one and only, the eternal, the absolute, and incomparable. Although in Islam God is beyond our human "knowing" or comprehension, the tradition has nevertheless used a range of images, attributes, or names for God, such as "Creator," "Mighty," "Wise," "The Compassionate," or "The Merciful." Indeed, alongside formal prayer, Islam has included a wider practice of recalling or silently reciting the names for God during the day (*dhikr*). God is the creator of everything that exists, simply by divine command. Therefore, material creation is a reflection of God, through which God may be "known," and its purpose is to worship God and to give glory to God.[18]

Beyond the three Abrahamic religions, the use of positive images or language about the divine is arguably most obviously present in certain forms of Hinduism. For example, the school of Vaishnavism uses positive language about the nature and qualities of the Supreme Lord Krishna or Vishnu. The yogic tradition is more ambiguous. The Yoga Sutras of Patanjali not only suggested a range of spiritual practices, but in its underlying philosophy defined yoga as countering the "perturbation of the mind" as a necessary condition for us to rise above intellectual reasoning. On the other hand, in the Hindu text the Bhagavad Gita, one type of yoga, Jnana yoga, is said to support the acquisition of knowledge of the Divine.[19]

18. On mysticism in Islam, see e.g., Annemarie Schimmel, *Mystical Dimensions of Islam* (Chapel Hill: University of North Carolina Press, 1983). For an overview summary of Islamic mysticism, see Sheldrake, *Spirituality: A Guide for the Perplexed*, chapter 7. For a wider overview of spirituality in Islam, see the essays by different authors in the two volumes of *Islamic Spirituality*, ed. Seyyed Hossain Nasr (New York: Crossroad, 1991).

19. For an overview of Hindu spirituality, see, e.g., Arvind Sharma, *A Guide to Hindu Spirituality* (Bloomington, IN: World Wisdom, 2006).

The tradition of Buddhism is, overall, nontheistic rather than overtly atheistic. The Buddha seems to have taught that there is no creator God who saves us and on whom we are wholly dependent. In that context, Buddhist knowing and unknowing do not refer to our relationship with God. Overall, the Buddha consciously avoided the theoretical doctrines of other religions. However, knowing and unknowing are not entirely absent. The Buddha's teachings were a recipe for all "sentient beings" to be freed from the suffering of material existence, to escape the inevitable cycle of birth and rebirth which is a result of our ignorance, and to achieve ultimate enlightenment (*nirvāna*). The ideal of enlightenment implies that we eventually overcome ignorance about the true nature of reality and of our existence. Thus, *nirvāna* is the ultimate extinction of suffering in a state of knowing or enlightenment about the true nature of reality. In this state, the independent self is recognized as an illusion. *Nirvāna* is not an encounter with a transcendent God but is the absence of all separate identity and thus is the achievement of ultimate tranquility through being united with true knowledge and with our true nature.[20]

Finally, a quest for hidden knowledge of reality is a characteristic of what are known as "esoteric movements" outside traditional religions, such as Theosophy and Anthroposophy. Apart from secret rituals and special initiates, many esoteric spiritualities embrace a quest for illuminated knowledge based on an interconnection between the visible and invisible universe. In some respects, the esoteric movements are associated with the mystical because of the widespread emphasis on hidden knowledge and superior illumination. For example, Theosophy, founded by Madame Blavatsky in the late nineteenth

---

20. For an overview of Buddhist spirituality, see the two multiauthor volumes edited by Takeuchi Yoshinori, *Buddhist Spirituality: Indian, Southeast Asian, Tibetan, Early Chinese* (New York: Crossroad Publishing, 1995) and *Buddhist Spirituality: Later China, Korea, Japan, and the Modern World* (New York: Crossroad Publishing, 1999).

century, overtly mixes mystical teachings, partly influenced by her exposure to Indian religions. Theosophy influenced the famous Russian composer Alexander Scriabin, who developed a mystic theory of music related to the transformation of perception. Equally, Anthroposophy, founded in the late nineteenth century by the Austrian thinker Rudolph Steiner, was based on a belief in a spiritual world which was accessible and led to deeper knowledge. This influenced the mystic vision of the artist Wassily Kandinsky. I will return to Anthroposophy and Steiner in chapter 6 on "Mysticism and Everyday Practice."

Conclusion

In our present times, there is a great curiosity about mysticism in Western countries. This is a recognizable part of postmodern religiosity. It seems to express a desire for immediate contact with the spiritual and the transcendent, however that is understood. The transcendent is presumed to be beyond what is often thought of as the cold objectivity of the life and teachings of institutional religion.[21] Mystics of every age—and every religion—have understood that the way to true understanding and fulfillment is a way of "unknowing" and dispossession. In the memorable words of the sixteenth-century Spanish mystic and poet, John of the Cross:

21. See, e.g., Carlo Carozza, "Mysticism and the Crisis of Religious Institutions," in "Mysticism and the Institutional Crisis," ed. Christian Duquoc and Gustavo Gutierrez, *Concilium* 4 (1994): 17–26. However, in an important and complex study, Denys Turner questions the modern concept of mysticism that refers to a certain kind of experience and is the creation of nineteenth- and twentieth-century theorists. He suggests that the apophatic tradition did not expound subjective mysticism in this sense. See Denys Turner, *The Darkness of God: Negativity in Christian Mysticism* (Cambridge: Cambridge University Press, 1995), especially the introduction and chapter 11, "From Mystical Theology to Mysticism."

To reach satisfaction in all
   desire its possession in nothing.
To come to possess all
   desire the possession of nothing.
To arrive at being all
   desire to be nothing.
To come to the knowledge of all
   desire the knowledge of nothing.[22]

The postmodern affirmation that all religious language is relative reminds us that religious definitions are to be treated as provisional. The reality we name as "God" or "the Transcendent" exists beyond all categories—even beyond the familiar category of Being.[23] It is a central belief of Christianity that God is not ultimately definable and cannot be "known" in terms of rational thinking. Yet, as mystics of every age have intuitively grasped, a God who is Love may be touched in the here and now through our deep desire and longing love.

---

22. John of the Cross, *The Ascent of Mount Carmel*, Book 1, chapter 13, no. 11, in *The Collected Works of St. John of the Cross*, ed. Kieran Kavanaugh and Otilio Rodriguez (Washington, DC: Institute of Carmelite Studies, 1979).

23. On God and the category of "Being," see Jean-Luc Marion, *God without Being*, ET (Chicago: University of Chicago Press, 1995), especially chapter 3.

CHAPTER FIVE

WONDER AND BEAUTY

There is an intense relationship between a deepened sense of beauty or wonder and mystical experience and illumination. This is especially noticeable in what is known as "nature mysticism" but also in the worlds of music, art, and poetry. The present chapter will briefly explore this third approach to mysticism.

BEAUTY AND AESTHETICS

Even in nonreligious contexts, beauty and aesthetics have become an important medium for "the spiritual." The origins of the word "aesthetics" lie in the ancient Greek *aisthetikos*—that is, "concerning perception." This implies that we come to understand even the hidden depths of reality through our bodily senses. In this context, beauty is not merely concerned with what is immediately attractive. Rather, beauty connects with "the sublime" or sacred, with truth, and with moral integrity. Apart from nature, the imagery of art, music, and poetry has the power to communicate meaning through our imagination. The great Italian scholar Umberto Eco, in his stimulating book on beauty, noted that the importance of "clarity" in approaches to aesthetics in ancient and in medieval thought derived from the notion that God is identified with light. In pre-Roman times, the many gods were frequently seen as personifications of the sun. Umberto Eco suggested that this theme passed into Christianity via the philosophy of Neoplatonism. The light that shines upon us reflects the supreme and unattainable One from whom all light emanates. Thus, God is identified as a kind of luminous current that permeates the universe.[1]

Beauty, imagination, and the arts also play a role in religious experience. Patristic theology (for example, Augustine), medieval theology (for example, Thomas Aquinas), and some modern theologians (for example, Hans Urs von Balthasar) saw God as the source of all earthly beauty. Beauty finds its perfection in God. All created beauty, whether nature, art, music, or poetry, reflects and participates to some degree in the beauty of the Divine. Beauty in ancient philosophy (for example, Plato and Aristotle) was not merely concerned with aesthetics but was also related to moral goodness.[2] The eighteenth-century philosopher Immanuel Kant connected aesthetics with a wider philosophy of beauty. The idea of beauty was to be associated with the notion of "the sublime"—that is, with what is awe-inspiring in nature, art, and human thought. Other late Romantic theorists also linked "the sublime" explicitly with "the holy."

THE MYSTICISM OF NATURE

I want to begin by exploring the connection between nature and the mystical. The concept of "nature mysticism" engages with such natural elements as the ocean, mountains, or wilderness. These evoke a sense of liminality—that is, we exist on the

---

1. See Umberto Eco, *On Beauty: A History of a Western Idea*, ET (London: Secker & Warburg, 2004), chapter IV, "Light & Colour in the Middle Ages," Section 2, "God as Light," 102.

2. See the seven volumes of Hans Urs von Balthasar, *The Glory of the Lord: A Theological Aesthetics*, ET (San Francisco: Ignatius Press, 1982–1989); E. Farley, *Faith and Beauty: A Theological Aesthetic* (Aldershot: Ashgate, 2001); and R. Viladesan, *Theological Aesthetics: God in Imagination, Beauty, and Art* (Oxford: Oxford University Press, 1999).

boundary between the material world and the transcendent. The natural world, even its smallest features, enables us to develop a sense of profound wonder. In our current times of dangerous climate change, this highlights the vital importance of having a strong ecological consciousness.

Many people testify to intense spiritual experiences connected to their engagement with nature. Examples include solitude in wilderness hiking and in mountaineering. For some people, this is related to quasi-mystical "bliss" and a sense of oceanic interconnectedness. The rediscovery of "wild nature" is often associated with the nineteenth-century American Romantic movement, for example the writings of Henry Thoreau (1817–1862) and Ralph Waldo Emerson (1803–1882).

I begin my reflections on the power of nature, especially landscapes, to provoke a mystical deepening of our consciousness with my own experience. For some people, their surrounding landscape is nothing more than a backdrop to life. However, for others it becomes the medium for profound spiritual awareness. All of us have our preferred landscapes. Thus, some people are particularly drawn to deserts, forests, hills, mountains, or oceans. There is something about these landscapes that evokes within us a sense of awe. We sense that we are part of something far larger than our immediate context and feel connected to God, the transcendent, or the eternal. This experience is often recorded in relation to mountaineering. For example, climbing Mount Everest becomes an experience of "standing on top of the world," not merely literally but also spiritually. It is said that for the great climber George Mallory, who disappeared near the summit of Mount Everest in 1924 and whose body was only rediscovered in 1999, the mountain represented everything visionary and mystical.

In my own case, I grew up in England on the border between the semirural counties of Hampshire and Dorset. On one side of our town was the beautiful New Forest, a national park of unenclosed pasture, heathland, and forest, inhabited by many species of birds, as well as by wild ponies and deer. On the other side of town was the Dorset landscape of ancient hills filled with history (some of it associated with the legend of King Arthur). There were the remains of Bronze Age hill settlements, Celtic burial mounds, Roman forts, castles, medieval field systems, a myriad of medieval village churches, and pre-Reformation monastic remains. Even the familiar clumps of trees on local hilltops turned out to be related to pre-Christian sacred groves.

Currently, I am moved and filled with wonder whenever I listen to a particular piece of music by the English twentieth-century composer Ralph Vaughan Williams, "The Lark Ascending." This evocative music for violin and orchestra has strong echoes of the English countryside. It lifts my spirit back to earlier memories of the beautiful singing of birds, especially skylarks, the voice of English springtime. In recent years, I have regularly experienced the song of skylarks while walking on wild heathland next to the North Sea in the county of Suffolk, where some of my family have a house.

However, for me, more than any other part of nature, the sea is a powerful and evocative force. As a child I always lived close to the ocean and my school overlooked cliffs and beaches. We were taught that wild waves could be dangerous, but we also learned to trust ourselves to the sea as we swam or floated on the water while gazing up at the vast sky. A school friend of mine (who sadly died recently) also had a small sailing dinghy, and in our teenage years we regularly sailed together around the semi-enclosed local bay.

> Delightful I think it to be in the bosom of an isle, on the peak of a rock, that I might often see there the calm of the sea.
>
> That I might see its heavy waves over the glittering ocean, as they chant a melody to their Father on their eternal course.[3]

3. See K. Hurlstone Jackson, ed., *A Celtic Miscellany* (London: Penguin Classics, 1971), 279, no. 222.

These words from an ancient Celtic Christian source beautifully capture my experience of the constantly changing nature of the sea—whether flat calm or heavy waves, with the effect of light on water and the sound of the tide advancing on shingled beaches.[4]

The classic English writer on mysticism, Evelyn Underhill, noted that

> To "see God in nature," to attain a radiant consciousness of the "otherness" of natural things, is the simplest and commonest form of illumination. Most people, under the spell of emotion, or of beauty, have known flashes of rudimentary vision of this kind. Where such a consciousness is recurrent, as it is in many poets, there results that partial yet often overpowering apprehension of the Infinite Life immanent in all living things, which some modern writers have dignified by the name of "nature mysticism."[5]

The notion of "the Infinite Life immanent in all living things" takes us back to the sentiments of Celtic Christian spirituality, as well as to the riches of Francis of Assisi's hymn to creation in the early thirteenth century.

My first example is the sixth-century Irish monastic missionary Columbanus, who in one of his sermons affirmed unequivocally the presence of God in nature:

> Therefore God is everywhere, utterly vast, and everywhere nigh at hand, according to His own witness of

---

4. On spirituality and landscape, see, e.g., Belden Lane, *The Solace of Fierce Landscapes: Exploring Desert and Mountain Spirituality* (Oxford: Oxford University Press, 1998). Also see Philip Sheldrake, *Living Between Worlds: Place and Journey in Celtic Spirituality* (London: Darton, Longman & Todd, 1996), chapter 2, "Landscape and Sacred Sites," and chapter 6, "The Natural World"; and Philip Sheldrake, *Spaces for the Sacred: Place Memory and Identity* (London: SCM Press, 2001), chapter 1, "A Sense of Place."

5. Evelyn Underhill, *Mysticism: The Nature and Development of Spiritual Consciousness* (1930; repr., London: Oneworld Publications, 1993), 234.

Himself; I am, He says, a God at hand and not a God
afar off . . .

Seek no further concerning God; for those who wish to
know the great deep must first review the natural world.[6]

There is also a wonderful prayer that is part of a collection
gathered from the Gaelic-speaking parts of Scotland and the
islands of the Hebrides. This powerfully links the presence of
God to the world of nature.

There is no plant in the ground
But is full of His virtue,
There is no form in the strand
But is full of His blessing.

There is no bird on the wing,
There is no star in the sky,
There is nothing beneath the sun,
But proclaims His goodness.[7]

Moving forward to the thirteenth century, one of the most
famous expressions of the spiritual, even mystical, qualities
embedded in the natural world is the Canticle of Creation by
Francis of Assisi. What is the meaning of the Canticle? While
it is possible to reduce it simply to a romantic love of nature,
the underlying message of the Canticle is far deeper. Francis
of Assisi's teaching is that all our fellow creatures (whether
people, animals, or natural features of the landscape) are our
sisters and brothers and reflect the face of Jesus Christ. Francis's experience was that every element of creation comes from
the same source, that is, God as revealed in the incarnation.

6. See G. S. M. Walker, ed., *Sancti Columbani Opera* (Dublin: 1970),
Sermon I, 63 and 65.
7. Alexander Carmichael, ed., *Carmina Gadelica*, vol. 1 (Edinburgh:
Oliver & Boyd, 1992), 39–41.

Thus, we come to know God through all aspects of creation. The foundation of Francis's respect for all created things is that the God who created everything has come among us in the person of Jesus of Nazareth, known as the Christ. Francis's Canticle speaks of the cosmic solidarity of all creation, for example:

> Let everything you have made
> Be a song of praise to you,
> Above all, our Sister, our Mother, Lady Earth
> Who feeds and rules and guides us.
> Through her you give us fruits and flowers
> Rich with a million hues.
> O my Lord, be praised.[8]

One of the followers of Francis of Assisi, the thirteenth-century Franciscan friar John Duns Scotus, was an outstanding Scottish philosopher and theologian. Duns Scotus taught at Oxford and in Paris. He was deeply influenced by Francis of Assisi's spirituality, not least the Canticle of Creation. Duns Scotus expressed his thought most originally in the concept of "particularity." This offers a positive view of everything that is specific and individual in creation, even the smallest thing. By implication, Duns Scotus taught that, without exception, every element in nature in its very particularity has a unique and irreplaceable value. This is because everything participates directly in the life of God the Creator. Each particular material element is a unique expression of God's own beauty. For example, to the category of "leaf" and of "tree" is added an individualizing form that makes it specific. It is *this* leaf and *this* tree. On this basis, a particular leaf cannot simply be replaced

8. Modern translation from the medieval Italian by the English Poor Clare scholar, Sr. Frances Teresa. See her *Living the Incarnation: Praying with Francis and Clare of Assisi* (London: Darton, Longman & Todd, 1993), 129.

by another leaf. Duns Scotus gave the name *haecceitas*, "this-ness," to the particularity of each element of creation.[9]

Later, during the seventeenth century, the Anglican priest Thomas Traherne was an outstanding English spiritual writer. He was also a mystic in the opinion of many. Traherne's writings have come back into focus in recent years. There is no evidence that he was directly influenced by Duns Scotus. However, Traherne shares many of Duns Scotus's sentiments in relation to creation and nature. Traherne is best known for his book, *Centuries of Meditations*, a collection of short paragraphs in which he reflects on the Christian life.[10] Traherne frequently explores the glory of creation in relation to his own intimate relationship with God. For example, in "The First Century," there are a range of profound sentiments regarding the spiritual quality of even the smallest things in the natural world.

> Your enjoyment of the World is never right, till you so esteem it, that everything in it, is more your treasure than a King's exchequer full of Gold and Silver. And that exchequer yours also in its place and service. Can you take too much joy in your Father's works? He is Himself in everything. ("First Century," no. 25)

> You never enjoy the world aright, till you see how a sand exhibiteth the wisdom and power of God. ("First Century," no. 27)

> Your enjoyment of the world is never right, till every morning you awake in Heaven; see yourself in your Father's Palace; and look upon the skies, the earth, and the air as Celestial Joys. ("First Century," no. 28)

9. See, e.g., Thomas Williams, ed., *The Cambridge Companion to Duns Scotus* (Cambridge: Cambridge University Press, 2002).

10. See, e.g., H. M. Margoliouth, ed., *Thomas Traherne: Centuries* (Oxford: Mowbray, 1975).

> Yet further, you never enjoy the world aright, till you so love the beauty of enjoying it, that you are covetous and earnest to persuade others to enjoy it. ("First Century, no. 31)

Further in Traherne's "Third Century" there is this powerful passage:

> The corn was orient and immortal wheat, which never should be reaped, nor was ever sown. I thought it had stood from everlasting to everlasting. The dust and stones of the street were as precious as gold: the gates were at first the end of the world. The green trees when I saw them first through one of the gates transported and ravished me, their sweetness and unusual beauty made my heart to leap, and almost mad with ecstasy, they were such strange and wonderful things. ("Third Century, no. 3)

During the nineteenth century, the outstanding English poet Gerard Manley Hopkins was explicitly and strongly influenced by the thought of Duns Scotus while he studied at Oxford. Hopkins was received into the Roman Catholic Church in 1866 by John Henry Newman. He then became a Jesuit priest and ended up as a professor at University College Dublin. His poem "Duns Scotus's Oxford" affirms:

> Yet ah! This air I gather and I release
> He lived on; these weeds and waters, these walls are what
> He haunted who of all men most sways my spirits to peace

It is clear from his journals that the glories of nature were always important to Gerard Manley Hopkins. Beauty was the principle behind all that exists. Hopkins's senses led him to a quasi-mystical illumination about created reality that he called "inscape." "Inscape" refers to the distinctive design that gives each individual natural element its particular identity. This identity is not something static but is dynamic in the sense that every created element in the universe "selves" (in Hopkins' words) and thus enacts its identity.

In one of his best-known poems, Hopkins affirms that nature is filled with the grandeur of God:

> The world is charged with the grandeur of God.
> It will flame out, like shining from shook foil;
> It gathers to a greatness, like the ooze of oil
> Crushed. Why do men then now not reck his rod?
> Generations have trod, have trod, have trod;
> And all is seared with trade; bleared, smeared with toil;
> And wears man's smudge and shares man's smell: the soil
> Is bare now, nor can foot feel, being shod.
>
> And for all this, nature is never spent;
> There lives the dearest freshness deep down things;
> And though the last lights off the black West went
> Oh, morning, at the brown brink eastward, springs—
> Because the Holy Ghost over the bent
> World broods with warm breast and with ah! Bright wings.[11]

Gerard Manley Hopkins is something of a paradox. He was a priest-poet who wanted to evoke the spiritual heart of nature and to do so in a sensuous way.

THE MYSTICAL IN THE ARTS

I now want to turn to the relationship between the arts and the mystical. In a fascinating collection of essays, *Art and the Spiritual,* some major contemporary artists and film directors, such as Antony Gormley, Bill Viola, and David Puttnam, engage with the interface of the arts and spirituality. All the writers believe that the spiritual power of art lies in the fact that, while it arises out of an engagement with the material

11. See Catherine Phillips, ed., *Mortal Beauty, God's Grace* (Oxford: Oxford University Press, 1986).

world, it also offers a deep spiritual sense of the wholeness of humanity and of the world.[12]

Along with music and poetry, the arts have the capacity to evoke the transcendent, to provoke reverence and a transgression of material boundaries and also to touch the depths of human awareness. For example, there is great spiritual depth in the art of Michelangelo, in the poetry of George Herbert, or in the music of Johann Sebastian Bach. The great twentieth-century German theologian Karl Rahner also argued that in the arts what is genuinely spiritual appears beyond the boundaries of conventional religion. For example, Rahner wrote of the "anonymous reverence" of French Impressionism, many of whose representatives were at best agnostics rather than conventional religious believers.[13]

The arts have been relatively neglected in Christian theology. There are a number of reasons for this. For example, some people have considered art to be essentially seductive and sensual, to overindulge human emotion and to be more concerned with entertaining the viewer than with anything deeper. However, outside formal theology, the Christian tradition has itself made significant use of the arts—not least in iconography, in the design of church buildings, or in the performance of worship.

At the heart of all the arts—for example painting, music, and poetry—is the power of the image. The artist, composer, or poet creates an image and communicates via imagery. We then receive the meaning they seek to communicate to us through our imagination. Artistic, musical, and poetic images have the capacity to touch our spiritual depths beyond the limits of rational language and mere description.

12. B. Hall and D. Jaspers, eds., *Art and the Spiritual* (Sunderland: University of Sunderland Press, 2003).

13. See Karl Rahner, "Art against the Horizon of Theology and Piety," in his *Theological Investigations*, vol. 23 (London: Darton, Longman & Todd, 1992), 162–68.

Historically, a creative art such as painting has deep religious roots. The role of art as a spiritual and mystical statement or medium is explicit in some religious traditions. One important example is the tradition of iconography in Eastern Orthodox Christianity. An outstanding—and famous—example is the icon of the Trinity painted by the fifteenth-century Russian iconographer Andrei Rublev. Overall, this icon is thought to be one of the greatest expressions of Russian art. The important point is that the role of icons is not purely aesthetic. Icon paintings are explicitly spiritual because each icon is believed to be a medium of divine power and communication that has a spiritual impact on each person when they contemplate it or pray in front of it. In a quasi-mystical understanding, Eastern Orthodox Christianity believes that through our spiritual interaction with icons, we may become united with what the icon represents—for example, the Trinity as in Rublev's icon, or Jesus Christ, the Virgin Mary, or some other saints.

In Western art, one of the most overtly spiritual artists was the sixteenth-century and early seventeenth-century painter Domenikos Theotokopoulos. He is better known as El Greco because of his Cretan-Greek origins prior to arriving in Spain via Rome. El Greco experienced the mystical inner structure of life. Many of his works reflect the mysticism and spiritual fervor of the religious revival in Spain as a result of the Catholic Reformation. El Greco may have come from the Eastern Orthodox tradition before aligning with Western Catholicism. He was certainly influenced by the Orthodox tradition of icons, in which it seems he trained. However, El Greco is also seen as echoing the Carmelite mysticism of Teresa of Avila and John of the Cross. Angelic and human figures are portrayed by El Greco in his paintings as losing themselves in ecstatic experience.[14]

14. See James Romaine, "El Greco's Mystical Vision," October 22, 2003, https://oldarchive.godspy.com/culture/El-Grecos-Mystical-Vision.cfm.htm.

Outside formal religion, I have already mentioned Karl Rahner's comments about the "anonymous" spiritual qualities of Impressionism. However, several twentieth-century artists explicitly saw their art as an expression of a spiritual vision, a way of trying to touch the transcendent and, in itself, a form of spiritual practice. For example, the artist Wassily Kandinsky, influenced by Rudolph Steiner and the movement of esoteric philosophy known as Anthroposophy, suggested that "to send light into the darkness of men's hearts—such is the duty of the artist." Another twentieth-century artist, Piet Mondrian, believed that artists were only able to attain their artistic ideal by reaching a point where there was direct and conscious interaction with "the spiritual."

Historically, another artistic form with powerful spiritual resonances is architecture. Whether we think, for example, of the ancient mosques in the Middle East, the great medieval European cathedrals, or the extraordinary Meenakshi Amman Hindu temple in the Indian city of Madurai, religious buildings have historically offered a treasury of spiritual meaning and have also given a sacred focus to city landscapes. One striking example of the spiritual power of religious buildings is the continued fascination with the great medieval cathedrals of Western Europe, even in a supposedly post-religious age. Cathedrals continue to attract large numbers of visitors. Contemporary research suggests that most visitors do not treat such buildings simply as historical monuments but find in them a sense of the sacred. Many people have a genuinely spiritual experience when they visit cathedrals today. The original theory behind the architecture of medieval cathedrals was overtly spiritual and, indeed, quasi-mystical. In these great churches, paradise was evoked and expressed in material terms in the design, layout, and artwork. To enter the cathedral was to be transported into a transcendent realm by its space, light, color, and architectural design. The architecture of the medieval cathedrals was explicitly intended to be a microcosm of the cosmos that would draw the pilgrim into an encounter with the transcendent realm.[15]

Music and the Mystical

Another artistic medium, music, plays an important role in all the major world religions. While it often accompanies the performance of religious rituals, it is sometimes also considered to be a spiritual or mystical expression in and of itself. Indeed, some religious music, such as recordings of the ethereal sound of Gregorian chant sung by Western monastic communities, has an enthusiastic following among people who do not otherwise identify as religious. I recall being at a wedding reception some years ago where someone in my group mentioned that he was not religious but relaxed at the end of every working day by listening to recordings of monastic Gregorian chant. Others in the group then said the same.

An outstanding medieval example of music related to the mystical is the work of the twelfth-century German aristocratic Benedictine abbess Hildegard of Bingen. Hildegard was a visionary mystic (for example, in her text *Scivias*) and a prophetic reformist in the church and in wider society. She was a prolific writer across a range of disciplines, an expert in herbal medicine, an artist, and a poet. However, Hildegard was also a talented musician who composed more than seventy spiritual songs, including their distinctive music. Hildegard has attracted a large contemporary following, not all of whom are conventionally religious.

15. For more detailed comments on the spiritual-theological-mystical language of medieval cathedral architecture, see, e.g., my books *Spaces for the Sacred: Place, Memory and Identity* (Baltimore: Johns Hopkins University Press, 2001), 51–61; and *The Spiritual City: Theology, Spirituality and the Urban* (Malden, MA: Wiley Blackwell, 2014), 65–69. Also, see my article "Reading Cathedrals as Spiritual Texts," in *Studies in Spirituality* 11 (Titus Brandsma Institute: Nijmegen, Netherlands, 2001), 187–204.

Several twentieth-century composers also engaged overtly with the spiritual. The French examples stand out. For example, Olivier Messiaen, one of the major composers of the twentieth century and a deeply religious person, believed that sound was itself spiritual because it connected us to the harmonies of the cosmos. For much of his adult life, Messiaen was a church organist in Paris, as well as teaching at the Paris Conservatoire. Other French composers who touched upon the spiritual and the mystical include Maurice Duruflé, an organist whose famous Requiem was strongly influenced by Gregorian chant, and another organist-composer Jehan Alain, who was influenced by both Debussy and Messiaen. He was killed at the Battle of Saumur in 1940, aged only twenty-nine, and posthumously awarded the Croix de Guerre. One of Alain's most famous organ pieces was "Litanies," of which he said, "When, in its distress, the Christian soul can find no more words to invoke God's mercy, it repeats endlessly the same litany. For reason has reached its limit. Only faith can take one further."

Other examples of music connected to the mystical include the American composer John Cage, who based his abstract style of music on Buddhist spiritual teachings, and the Estonian Arvo Pärt, a leading minimalist composer. Pärt is considered by some commentators to be the greatest living classical composer. A convert from Lutheranism to Eastern Orthodoxy, Pärt is inspired both by Western monastic plainchant and by the music of the Orthodox Church.

Spiritual experience has also impacted on elements of European musical theatre. An outstanding example is the Musik-TheaterKöln, which has used mystical texts, both Buddhist and Christian. For example, in terms of Buddhism, Zen koans from the Mu Mon Kwan (or Mumonkan), a thirteenth-century Chinese text, have been the basis for one musical. In relation to Christian mysticism, the chamber opera *Las Canciones* was based on the poetry of the sixteenth-century Spanish mystic

John of the Cross. The opera sought, through text and music, to express the surrender of the human spirit to God.

Two twentieth-century English composers are also notable for their engagement with the mystical. The first, Gerald Finzi, wrote a wide range of music but is perhaps best known for his choral pieces. Despite being an agnostic of Jewish descent, several of Finzi's choral works incorporate Christian texts. For example, in the aftermath of the First World War, during which he lost his music teacher and three of his brothers, Finzi found great solace in the poetry of the Anglican mystic Thomas Traherne. His 1939 cantata for solo soprano or tenor and string orchestra used three of Traherne's overtly mystical poems, plus the extract I quoted earlier from Traherne's "Third Century" in his *Centuries of Meditation*.

Ralph Vaughan Williams was one of the greatest English composers of the twentieth century who wrote an extensive range of music. While the son of an Anglican priest, Vaughan Williams was, like Finzi, an open-minded agnostic who nevertheless wrote beautiful religious choral music. His work "Five Mystical Songs" sets to music poems by George Herbert, the outstanding seventeenth-century English poet and Anglican priest in whom the composer saw a mystical sensibility. The music is for a baritone soloist plus various choices for accompaniment. The choice used at the premiere conducted by the composer included orchestra and chorus. Vaughan Williams uses four of Herbert's poems, with one poem, "Easter," divided into two halves, for the first two mystical songs. The third song, conventionally entitled in Herbert collections as "Love 3," begins with the line "Love bade me welcome." This is the poem that strongly impacted the religiously unconventional figure Simone Weil. She was introduced to Herbert's poetry by a visitor from England while spending Easter at the Abbey of Solesmes just before the Second World War. She then used "Love 3" regularly for meditation, and it seems to have been the medium for a powerful mystical experience of the presence of Christ.

Love bade me welcome: yet my soul drew back
　　Guilty of dust and sin.
But quick-ey'd Love, observing me grow slack
　　From my first entrance in,
Drew nearer to me, sweetly questioning,
　　If I lack'd anything.

A guest, I answer'd, worthy to be here:
　　Love said, you shall be he.
I the unkind, ungrateful? Ah my dear,
　　I cannot look on thee.
Love took my hand, and smiling did reply,
　　Who made the eyes but I?

Truth Lord, but I have marr'd them: let my shame
　　Go where it doth deserve.
And know you not, says Love, who bore the blame?
　　My dear, then I will serve.
You must sit down says Love, and taste my meat:
So I did sit and eat. ("Love 3")

I will now turn in more detail to further expressions of the
mystical in poetry.

POETRY AND THE MYSTICAL

　　The mystical is powerfully expressed in some religious poetry, as I have already mentioned. Returning first of all to
George Herbert and Vaughan Williams's powerful musical
settings of "Five Mystical Songs," one of the other songs is
Herbert's poem entitled "The Call." The words of this poem
are also used as a hymn in several different Christian traditions:

Come, my Way, my Truth, my Life:
Such a Way, as gives us breath:
Such a Truth, as ends all strife:
And such a Life, as killeth death.

Come, my Light, my Feast, my Strength:
Such a Light, as shows a feast:
Such a Feast, as mends in length:
Such a Strength, as makes his guest.

Come, my Joy, my Love, my Heart:
Such a Joy as none can move:
Such a Love, as none can part:
Such a Heart, as joys in love.

However, for me one of George Herbert's most striking poems which touches the mystical is entitled Prayer 1. This does not appear in Vaughan Williams's musical selection. Prayer is richly portrayed as our ongoing—and complex—relationship with God, rather than in terms of methods and spiritual practices.

Prayer the Church's banquet, Angels' age,
God's breath in man returning to his birth,
The soul in paraphrase, heart in pilgrimage,
The Christian plummet sounding heav'n and earth;
Engine against th'Almighty, sinners' tower,
Reversed thunder, Christ-side-piercing spear,
The six-days-world transposing in an hour,
A kind of tune, which all things hear and fear;
Softness, and peace, and joy, and love, and bliss,
Exalted Manna, gladness of the best,
Heaven in ordinary, man well drest,
The milky way, the bird of Paradise,
Church-bells beyond the stars heard, the soul's blood,
The land of spices, something understood.

This is an extraordinary poem, even in its literary construction. It is a sonnet yet has no main verb. It is simply a succession of brief and powerful metaphorical phrases. As a result, the poem's effect is cumulative rather than offering a conclusive definition of prayer. In attempting to express the nature of prayer, Herbert turns away from the obvious path of simile, that is, "prayer is like . . . " Herbert's use of metaphors offers greater imaginative scope that enables him to draw the reader beyond the limits of what can be expressed, let alone conclusively defined. Paradoxically, therefore, Herbert offers many images of prayer-as-relationship; yet he also suggests the deep underlying truth that our relationship with God is ultimately beyond our ability to express simply in human words. It is a mysterious process that enables people to touch ultimate Mystery. Herbert's range of metaphors swings between time and eternity, the everyday and heaven. In just the same way prayer acts as a bridge between two worlds—the world of the everyday and the eternal world of heaven.

The poem begins with the phrase "Prayer the Church's Banquet." As we might expect in Herbert, all prayer is common prayer, the prayer of the church. The metaphor has another dimension as well. A banquet is a meal. This suggests that prayer is spiritual food—a metaphor deepened by others later in the poem such as "exalted manna" and "land of spices."

Prayer is also deeply personal. It is "the soul's blood," that is, the source of life coursing through our veins. It is also "the soul in paraphrase": it expands the soul to its full potential and is the most perfect expression of our deepest self. "God's breath in man returning to his birth" suggests that prayer-as-relationship is in some way God's action within us and has the capacity to return people to the first moment of creation, the source of all life as created by God.

The richness of the poem's imagery and its sensuous quality may give the impression that prayer is merely "softness, and peace, and joy, and love, and bliss." However, hints of spiritual struggle save the poem from feeling out of touch with the complexity and, at times, confusion of human experience. "Engine against th' Almighty" speaks of prayer as laying siege to God. This is an ambiguous image that suggests both perseverance and confrontation. Elsewhere, Herbert is not afraid to admit that he frequently battles with God. In this sense of struggle with God, Herbert echoes the spiritual tone of his beloved book of Psalms.

In the phrase "Heart in pilgrimage," George Herbert suggests that, through the medium of prayer, the depths of a person travel to another, transcendent, realm. Underlying Herbert's spiritual journey is an experience of transformation whereby an instinctive fear of God's wrath gives way to a realization of God's loving acceptance. The graphic metaphor, "Christ-side-piercing spear" suggests that the wound in Christ's side becomes a space where we may safely deposit our messages to God.

As a result of his inner struggles, Herbert came to a profound sense that the world of everyday experience was filled with the presence of God. Through its powerful and cumulative use of images, the poem offers an extraordinarily rich vision of the sacred as something encountered within the ordinary and yet which carries us to another dimension. Natural and biblical allusions combine with strikingly original images ("Church-bells beyond the stars heard") to suggest that our everyday world is transfigured by the radiance of divine glory: "Heaven in ordinary."

Herbert's love of musical imagery appears on many occasions throughout his poetry. The next line speaks of prayer as "a kind of tune." In "The six-days-world transposing in an hour," prayer transposes the "six-days" everyday world into another "key." For George Herbert, in prayer we come as close to God as is possible in our present existence.

The poem concludes with a pregnant but elusive phrase, "something understood." In the end, prayer-as-relationship touches the ultimately undefinable depths of God. Our spiritual experience is a continuous journey. Yet there is a sense of depth in the phrase "something understood" which hints at mystical insight beyond images and beyond words. The concluding metaphor is a paradoxical climax to the poem because it leaves the reader without a final definition. It is deliberately open-ended. "Something understood" is not the result of intellectual exploration but something that is tentative and incomplete yet also deeply mystical. In this "something" there is a hint that beyond the boundaries of our present awareness lie the hope and promise of a final completion. There is an ultimate vision of God which George Herbert's poem ends by affirming and celebrating.

Turning back to the sixteenth century, the great Spanish Carmelite mystic, John of the Cross, is also considered to be both a beautiful poet, as well as one of the greatest Spanish poets. In his work *The Living Flame of Love*, John of the Cross offers words that he suggests the soul recites in intimate and mystical union with God.[16] The first stanza, "Oh llama de amor viva," translates into English as:

> O living flame of love
> That tenderly wounds my soul
> In its deepest center! Since
> Now you are not oppressive,
> Now Consummate! If it be your will:
> Tear through the veil of this sweet encounter!

Along with the imagery of ecstatic fire and burning flames of love, John of the Cross uses water imagery in relation to fountains or springs and rivers—for example, in *The Spiritual Canticle*, which was inspired by the conversation between Bride and Bridegroom in the Song of Songs. Stanza 12 of his poem, "Oh cristalina fuente," translates as:

16. For an edition of the Spanish text, see Kathleen Jones, ed., *The Poems of St. John of the Cross* (Tunbridge Wells: Burns & Oates, 1993), 42–44. This edition offers an English translation, but a more accurate literal translation is the one I quote from Kieran Kavanaugh, ed., *John of the Cross: Selected Writings*, Classics of Western Spirituality (Mahwah, NJ: Paulist Press, 1987), 293–94.

> O spring-like crystal!
> If only, on your silvered-over face,
> You would suddenly form
> The eyes I have desired,
> Which I bear sketched deep within my heart.

Interestingly, it has been suggested by some scholars that the imagery of fire, flames, fountains, and flowing water reflects the impact of Al Andalus Sufi mysticism on John of the Cross, along with its influence on other late medieval and early modern Spanish Christian spiritual writers.[17]

Another Christian writer who was unquestionably influenced by Sufism was the Lebanese poet and artist Kahlil Gibran (1883–1931). He is also considered by some to have been a mystic. The work for which Kahlil Gibran is best known, which is arguably his masterpiece, is entitled *The Prophet*. This is a short collection of prose poems written in English. One of the sections speaks powerfully of beauty in a quasi-mystical way. The section begins:

> And a poet said, Speak to us of Beauty.
> And he answered:
> Where shall you seek beauty, and how shall you find her
> unless she herself be your way and your guide?
> And how shall you speak of her except she be the weaver
> of your speech?

The poem then offers various responses to this question—by the "aggrieved and injured," by "the tired and the weary," by "the watchmen of the city" and, finally, in winter by "the snowbound." Then the Prophet who is the wise man portrayed in the poems concludes:

17. See, e.g., Luce Lopez-Baralt, *San Juan de la Cruz y el Islam: Estudios sobre las Filiaciones Semiticas de su Literatura Mistica* (Madrid: Hiperion, 1990).

All these things have you said of beauty,
Yet in truth you spoke not of her but of needs unsatisfied,
And beauty is not a need but an ecstasy.
It is not a mouth thirsting nor an empty hand stretched forth,
But rather a heart enflamed and a soul enchanted.[18]

The connection between the Christian writer Kahlil Gibran and Sufi Islam brings me to two references to beauty that appear directly in Islamic mystical poetry.[19] In chronological order, first there is the late tenth-century and early eleventh-century CE Sufi sheikh (that is, teacher) Abu Said Ibn Abil-Khair from Iran.

Said I, "To whom belongs Thy Beauty?" He
Replied, "Since I alone exist, to Me;
Lover, Beloved and Love am I in one,
Beauty and Mirror, and the Eyes which see!"

Roughly a century later, another sheikh from Iran, also revered as a saint, is Ahmad Jam. Again, he addresses God as beauty:

Each who has seen Your beauty fine
Utters honestly, "I have seen the Divine."

Everywhere Your lovers wait for grace,
Remove Your veil, reveal Your face!

I am in the ocean and an ocean is in me;
This is the experience of one who can see.

He that leaps into the river of Unity,
He speaks of union with his Beloved's beauty.

18. See Kahlil Gibran, *The Prophet* (New York: Alfred A. Knopf, 2019), 74–75.

19. All the subsequent references are taken from Mahmood Jamal, ed., *Islamic Mystical Poetry: Sufi Verse from the Early Mystics to Rumi* (London: Penguin Books, 2009).

Finally, in the thirteenth century CE, there is Jalaluddin Rumi, who was born in what is now Afghanistan and is considered by many people to be the greatest mystical poet in Islamic literature.

> The time of Union
> Is the time of eternal Beauty.
> The time of favor and bounty
> Is the ocean of perfect purity.
>
> The wave of Bounty has appeared;
> The thunder of the sea arrived.
> The dawn of Blessedness had dawned.
> Not the Morn, it is the light of God
> That's dawned!

CONCLUSION

At the beginning of this chapter, I mentioned the book on beauty by Umberto Eco. He suggests that Christianity identifies God as the current of light that illuminates the universe. God is light. The light that we experience materially is therefore a reflection of the divine light from whom all other light arises. The same may be said of beauty. The Sufi mystics whom I quoted saw material beauty as a reflection of the divine. As Francis of Assisi reminds us, all created things reflect God. While this obviously refers to nature, it also applies to art, music, and poetry. As I have suggested throughout this chapter, their beauty has a deep spiritual quality that may evoke wonder and enable us to see, albeit imperfectly, the ultimate beauty that is God.

CHAPTER SIX

MYSTICISM AND
EVERYDAY PRACTICE

For some people, a relationship between mysticism and our practice of everyday life feels counterintuitive. This is because they interpret mysticism as essentially related to extraordinary experiences. However, in this chapter I suggest that the connection between mysticism and the everyday is an important aspect of a number of significant spiritual figures and spiritual writings in Christianity and also in other world faiths.

CHRISTIAN MYSTICISM AND THE EVERYDAY

In the Christian tradition, the relationship between mysticism and everyday life has sometimes been referred to as "a mysticism of everyday practice." This theme appears in different ways at a number of points throughout Christian history. However, the relationship between the mystical and radical social transformation, for example in liberation theology, will be the focus of chapter 7, "The Mystic as Radical Prophet."

In this present chapter, I mainly focus on three examples in Christianity. My main example is the spirituality of Ignatius Loyola, particularly expressed in his influential text, *The*

Spiritual Exercises—an important example of a "mysticism of everyday practice." My second brief, related example is the person of Mary Ward, an English Catholic nun from Yorkshire, who apparently received important mystical insights as a result of which she followed the practical spirituality of Ignatius Loyola. I will then turn my attention to a twentieth-century figure, Dag Hammarskjöld, the deeply spiritual (and arguably mystical) secretary general of the United Nations in the 1950s, and particularly his famous book *Markings*.

The chapter will conclude with an overview of mysticism and everyday practice in Judaism, Islam, Hinduism, and Buddhism.

IGNATIAN SPIRITUALITY

For me, an outstanding Christian example of the relationship between mysticism and the practice of everyday life is the highly influential sixteenth-century spiritual teacher, Ignatius Loyola. For many people, to call Ignatius Loyola a mystic or to affirm that Ignatian spirituality has a mystical dimension is something of a surprise. However, I suggest that unless we take the mystical side of Ignatius's spirituality seriously, we are in danger of turning Ignatius's spiritual teachings merely into a form of activism. Ignatius Loyola fully understood that everyday Christian action that is not based on deep contemplation and inner self-awareness is inevitably flawed.[1]

Ignatius Loyola (1491–1556), originally Iñigo Lopez de Loyola, is best known as the founder of the religious order known as the Society of Jesus (or Jesuits). He came from a noble family at Loyola in the Basque region of Spain and initially followed a military career that was conventional for a man

---

1. For references to Ignatius's writings and quotations in this chapter, see Joseph A. Munitiz, SJ, and Philip Endean, SJ, eds., *Saint Ignatius of Loyola: Personal Writings* (London: Penguin Classics, 2004). In the case of the *Spiritual Exercises*, references (e.g., Exx 1) are to the standard paragraph numbers used in all modern editions in every language.

of his social status. This ended when Ignatius was wounded in the 1521 defense of Pamplona against the French. He then underwent a conversion experience while recovering at his family castle. Subsequently, he lived as a hermit at Manresa near Barcelona (1522–23) and also worked at a local hospital. There he experienced mystical insights, received spiritual guidance from a Benedictine monk at the Abbey of Montserrat, and learned important lessons of spiritual discernment as he slowly overcame the temptation to indulge in excessive asceticism. The basic elements of his highly influential *Spiritual Exercises* were probably written at this time and then further refined by later experience of spiritually guiding other people, along with his theological studies in Paris.

After visiting the Holy Land, Ignatius began spiritual ministry in Spain and also studied at the universities of Alcalá and Salamanca (1524–1528). He gathered a group of followers, women and men, who sought to spread a spiritual message. As a result, Ignatius was investigated by the Inquisition, which was very suspicious of laypeople teaching or preaching in case they were secret heretics! More importantly, as we shall see, aspects of Ignatius's spirituality were based on what is known as the *Devotio Moderna* (or "Modern Devotion"), a late medieval semi-mystical spiritual renewal movement among laypeople and clergy originating in Northern Europe.

Ignatius eventually decided to study theology in Paris (1528–1535). There he gathered another group of like-minded male companions, as women were not allowed to attend university. They decided that forming a new religious order was the most effective way of promoting their spiritual ideals. By 1537, Ignatius and his companions were in Italy, and they obtained papal approval for their new order in 1540. The text of his *Spiritual Exercises* was formally approved in 1548. Ignatius then remained in Rome until his death as the first superior of the Society of Jesus, also writing copious letters of spiritual guidance to a varied audience of laypeople, both women and men, and clergy.

Ignatius's autobiography mentions that, while recovering from his Pamplona battle wounds, he meditated upon Jacobus de Voragine's lives of the saints and upon Ludolph of Saxony's *Life of Christ*—a text favored by the *Devotio Moderna* movement. Ludolph's introduction to his book suggested a form of gospel contemplation to enable a person to enter into scriptural scenes in an imaginative way. Visual contemplation became a key element of the *Exercises*. As we shall see, Ignatius adopted other spiritual practices from the *Devotio Moderna*. While at Manresa, he grew to love *The Imitation of Christ*, supposedly by Thomas à Kempis, which also relates to the *Devotio Moderna*. Ignatian scholars suggest that Ignatius was also influenced by the "spiritual exercises" of Abbot Cisneros of Montserrat (1455–1510), which were also influenced by the *Devotio Moderna*. Finally, while in Paris, Ignatius belonged to the Collège de Montaigu, founded by important figures in the *Devotio* movement.

Apart from the *Devotio Moderna*, other influences on Ignatius's spirituality remain a matter of debate. Much of his spiritual teaching was based on his own contemplative-mystical experiences, in addition to his guidance of other people. Ignatius also grew up in a Spanish culture influenced by centuries of Islamic presence, including a form of Sufism. This influence may be present in his *Spiritual Exercises*, including some spiritual practices derived from Sufi mysticism that also influenced other Christian mystics. I will return to this question later.

Apart from the *Spiritual Exercises*, two Ignatian texts are especially relevant in terms of Ignatius's mystical sensibilities. First, his *Spiritual Diary* mentions mystical illuminations—including visions of the Trinity—during six weeks in 1544, when he struggled to discern what God desired for the Jesuits in relation to a life of poverty. Second, Ignatius's dictated *Autobiography* or *Reminiscences*, that runs from his conversion in 1521 up to 1538, places great emphasis on an intimate relationship with God. As he struggled with his spiritual life, Ignatius described a vision of the Trinity as three keys on a keyboard (section 28), a vision of God creating the world (section 29), regular visions of the humanity of Christ and of Our Lady (also section 29), and reality transfigured in ways that illuminated his understanding of God and the world (section 30). He refers to seeing with "interior eyes." This phrase parallels the mystical language of his time. Here, as in the text of the *Exercises*, the emphasis is on a direct experience of God "in the heart," rather than through the intellect or religious observances. This mystical interiority underpins the *Spiritual Exercises*, with their practical and mission-oriented emphasis.

THE SPIRITUAL EXERCISES

I now want to mention a few specifics about the *Spiritual Exercises*, which is one of most influential spiritual texts of all times—nowadays used for spiritual guidance and retreats across an ecumenical range of Christians.[2] The text is not intended to be inspirational but is a series of practical notes for spiritual directors that suggest how to adapt the process to the needs of each person. The ideal is a month away from everyday pressures, but another form "in the midst of daily life" is also endorsed.[3] Much of the text consists of advice about the structure and content of meditation periods, guidance about spiritual discernment and making choices, and helpful remarks about practical matters related to the environment for prayer, the use of penance, eating, and dealing with scruples.

2. For a reliable introduction to Ignatian spirituality, which also underlines the central importance of discernment, see David Lonsdale, *Eyes to See, Ears to Hear: An Introduction to Ignatian Spirituality*, rev. ed. (Maryknoll, NY: Orbis Books, 2000). For a recent rereading of the Ignatian Exercises by women, which is also a helpful practical guidebook overall, see Katherine Dyckman, Mary Garvin, and Elizabeth Liebert, *The Spiritual Exercises Reclaimed: Uncovering Liberating Possibilities for Women* (New York: Paulist Press, 2001).

3. See *Spiritual Exercises* 19 and 20.

The explicit aim of the *Spiritual Exercises* is to help a person to grow in inner spiritual freedom in order to be able to respond to the call of Jesus Christ in everyday life. There are four phases, called Weeks, each with its specific focus, that enable the process to unfold. Alongside this structure, the actual spiritual dynamic will differ for each person. The First Week begins with human sin but in the context of a growing awareness of God's unwavering love. The retreatant is asked to recognize that God's call is addressed to all of us and that our unworthiness is no bar to responding. The Second Week deepens the sense of being called to "be with" Jesus Christ in mission through a series of gospel contemplations. This gradually leads retreatants to make a choice (or "Election") about their life. This is highlighted by three classic meditations on the contrasting values of Christ and worldliness: the "Two Standards" (Exx 136–48), the "Three Classes of Persons" (Exx 149–57) and the "Three Kinds of Humility" (Exx 165–68). Confronting Christ's values leads the retreatant to reflect on the cost of following him—expressed in the Third Week gospel meditations on Christ's suffering and death. By identifying with Christ's surrender to God, we may experience the joy and hope of the resurrection during what is known as the Fourth Week. The *Spiritual Exercises* end with a final "Contemplation for Attaining Love" (Exx 230–37) where everyday life is transformed into a context for finding God's presence working for us in all things.

From the *Spiritual Exercises*, it is possible to detect fundamental features of Ignatian spirituality and mysticism. First, God is encountered above all in everyday life which itself becomes a "spiritual exercise." Second, the life and death of Jesus Christ is the essential pattern for a Christian life. Third, God revealed in Christ offers healing, liberation, and hope. Fourth, spirituality is not so much a question of asceticism as of a deepening desire for God and an experience of God's loving acceptance in return. The theme of "finding God in all things" underpins a key Ignatian spiritual value of integrating contemplation and action. Following the way of Jesus Christ focuses on an active sharing in God's mission to the world—not least in serving people in need. Finally, at the heart of the spiritual journey is the gift of discernment—an increasing ability to judge wisely and to choose well in ways that are congruent with our deepest selves. I will return to discernment later in the chapter.

In terms of spiritual practices, I want to focus on four meditative practices which connect in different ways with a mystical sensibility. The first, known as "gospel contemplation," involves meditating on gospel passages that focus on the life and ministry of Jesus. The formula is laid out in two meditations at the beginning of Week Two, the "Contemplation on the Incarnation" (Exx 101–9) and the "Contemplation on the Nativity" (Exx 110–17). We first ask God that our meditation be directed only to God's purposes. Then we recall the relevant gospel scene and follow steps that derive ultimately from monastic *lectio divina*. A brief "composition of place" uses our imagination to enter the scriptural scene, while focusing intensely on what we desire. The main part of our meditation focuses on several "points" that enable us to reflect on the gospel narrative and personally to "draw fruit." Finally, contemplation ends with a "colloquy" (as in the *Devotio Moderna*)—an intense personal conversation with God "according to my inner feelings."

The second meditative practice is the "Application of the Senses." This is the final period of prayer in each day from Week Two. Its formula (Exx 121–26) is "to pass the five senses of the imagination" over key insights from earlier contemplations. It is a progressive contemplative simplification of prayer throughout the day. The *Devotio Moderna* meditation tradition suggested a movement from outer imagination to the "inner senses." For example, Geert Groote in his "Treatise on Four Classes of Subject Suitable for Meditation" sees this movement to the "inner senses" as contemplative and even mystical.[4] Thus, Ignatius's "application of the senses" leads a person beyond images to a form of infused contemplation.

The third meditative practice is known as the Examen. Once again, this short meditative review of each day derives from the *Devotio Moderna* movement (for example, Salome Sticken in her "Way of Life for Sisters" and Gerard Zerbolt in his "The Spiritual Ascents"). It appears in the *Spiritual Exercises* in two forms: the Particular Examen and the General Examen (Exx 24–43). There was a time when the Examen was seen as a moral exercise aimed at the correction of our faults. However, more recently its richer meaning has been recovered, not least by rediscovering its origins in the *Devotio Moderna*. The Examen is intended to be a contemplative review of each day. How did we respond to God in the midst of our daily life? This underlines two key Ignatian values. First, it deepens the contemplative process of "finding God in all things." Second, it sharpens our ability to exercise what Ignatius, and the longer Christian tradition, calls "discernment" or practical wisdom in relation to everyday choices. As we shall see, discernment in Ignatian spirituality concerns our ability, assisted by God, to recognize our different inner spiritual movements and desires and to be able to distinguish those that are life-giving from those that are destructive.

A fourth relevant Ignatian meditative practice is "The Third Way of Praying" (Exx 258–60). This appears in the "Additional Material" at the end of the *Exercises*. This spiritual practice is called variously "by rhythm" or "of the breath." The practice suggests taking a familiar prayer (for example, the Our Father) and linking each word in turn rhythmically to our breathing. Ignatius's sources for this practice are a mys-

---

4. Translations of Groote's text and the other texts cited from the *Devotio Moderna* are available in John Van Engen, ed., *Devotio Moderna: Basic Writings*, Classics of Western Spirituality (Mahwah, NJ: Paulist Press, 1988).

tery. Some scholars suggested connections with the Eastern Orthodox mystical movement known as hesychasm, especially the Jesus Prayer.[5] However, it is difficult to know how Ignatius would have encountered this tradition. Another possible source is a similar practice in Al-Andalus Sufi mysticism. It is now widely accepted that this form of Sufism influenced Jewish and Christian mysticism in Spain during the fifteenth and sixteenth centuries. Examples include Francisco de Osuna, Teresa of Avila, and John of the Cross, all of whom seem to have had Jewish roots.[6] Interestingly, several early Spanish Jesuit companions of Ignatius also had Jewish ancestry, such as Diego Lainez, the second Superior General of the Jesuits, and Juan de Polanco, Ignatius's secretary in Rome.[7]

THE MYSTICAL IN IGNATIUS'S SPIRITUALITY

In summary, there is significant evidence for a mystical dimension to Ignatius's spirituality of everyday practice, even though he avoided other prominent forms of mysticism in his day. For example, there is no evidence of the "nuptial" language of the Song of Songs that so strongly permeates Cistercian and Beguine mysticism. Nor is there the ambiguous God language employed by Rhineland mystics such as Meister Eckhart. Overall, it is difficult to detect the classical apophatic language of "unknowing" in Ignatius. Finally, while Ignatius does refer in the *Spiritual Exercises* to the first two

5. See Irenée Hausherr, "Les exercises spirituels de Saint Ignace et la méthode d'oraison hésychaste," *Orientalia Christiana Periodica*, no. 20 (1954): 7–26.

6. For a general study of such influences, see L. López-Baralt, *The Sufi 'trobar clus' and Spanish Mysticism: A Shared Symbolism* (Lahore, Pakistan: Iqbal Academy, 2000).

7. As noted by the French Jesuit scholar of Christian mysticism, Michel de Certeau, in his book *The Mystic Fable*, vol. 1 (Chicago: University of Chicago Press, 1992), 23.

contemplative-mystical stages—the purgative way and the illuminative way—he does not explicitly mention the way of union. However, some people suggest that Ignatius's emphasis on an intense immediacy in our relationship with God reflects an understanding of union with God that permeates the whole process of the *Spiritual Exercises* rather than being the final climactic "moment" of the spiritual journey.[8]

Throughout the *Spiritual Exercises*, Ignatius emphasizes the importance of experience, particularly the inner movements of the soul. The stress on "feeling and tasting things internally" (Exx 2) implicitly points to an understanding of God as dwelling and working within each person. The "Annotations" (or introductory remarks) at the beginning of the text insist that the one who gives the *Spiritual Exercises* to another person must not interfere with the direct inner relationship between God and the retreatant. On the contrary, the spiritual guide should "leave the Creator to work directly with the creature and the creature with the Creator and Lord" (Exx 15). We are to let

> The Creator and Lord communicate himself to the faithful soul in search for the will of God as he inflames her in his love and praise, disposing her towards the way in which she will be better able to serve him in the future. (Exx 15)

The final climax of the *Exercises*, the "Contemplation for Attaining Love" (Exx 230–37), posits a quasi-mystical transfiguration of our whole experience of reality. We are led to see everything in creation through God's eyes. We are invited to "see" or "find" God in all things, without exception, and conversely to see all things as flowing directly from God. While Ignatian spirituality as expressed in the *Spiritual Exercises* concerns mission and everyday practice, it also encourages the

---

8. For a study of Ignatius Loyola that underlines his mysticism, see Harvey Egan, *Ignatius the Mystic* (Wilmington, DE: Michael Glazier, 1987).

transformation of daily activity into an authentic "mysticism of practice" or of service. Becoming "people for others" in Ignatius is to be based on contemplative interiority and a resulting transformation of the self.

DISCERNMENT OF SPIRITS

A central aspect of Ignatian spirituality is discernment, which relates to how we make choices in life. I have already mentioned Ignatius's visionary experiences recorded in his *Spiritual Diary* in relation to his process of discernment about Jesuit spiritual values. For many people, choosing is purely pragmatic and discernment is essentially a process of working out the most effective way to live. However, in Ignatian spirituality, discernment is a much deeper, contemplative process. The word "discernment" means "to distinguish between things." In the Ignatian tradition, this involves the wisdom, inspired by God, to recognize the difference between desires and courses of action that are positively life-directing and others that are out of harmony with our relationship with God and with our true self.

Importantly, Ignatius's rules for discernment are more than just a way of interpreting inner spiritual experiences. They also concern finding God in the midst of ambiguous everyday realities. Daily life is itself a spiritual practice. As I have already mentioned, the great theme at the end of the *Spiritual Exercises*, "finding God in all things," involves a realization that God communicates with us in every aspect of our lives.

The word "discernment" derives from the Greek *diakrisis* and the Latin *discretio*, which have roots in ancient philosophy. The wisdom underpinning Ignatian discernment goes back to Aristotle's ethics, specifically Aristotle's third kind of knowledge—*phronesis* or "practical wisdom." While we know very little about the sources of Ignatius's spiritual teachings, it seems likely that, apart from his own spiritual experience, he learned about the longer discernment tradition while studying in Paris.

After all, Aristotle's ethics had a massive impact over the centuries on Western Christianity. His "practical wisdom" is the origin of "prudence," one of the seven "cardinal virtues." "Prudence" relates to decision-making—how to read our situations accurately and then respond wisely. For Aristotle, "practical wisdom" arises from our intuition, imagination, emotional engagement with life, and desire. "Desire" is also a central value in Ignatian spirituality.

For Aristotle, ethics (and Ignatian spirituality is profoundly ethical) is not simply a question of identifying good and bad actions. Aristotle is clear that humans need relationships with others. What is distinctive about being human is that our true fulfilment places certain demands upon us that do not always equate with purely individual choice. For Aristotle, authentic self-love relates to our quest for real friendship and for true society. This deeply fulfilled life is "noble" because it involves self-giving to other people.[9]

Crucially, neither Aristotle's practical wisdom nor Ignatian discernment are simply a matter of applying rules. They both refer to developing our underlying "character" or ways of being. A virtuous life involves choices that are aligned with our sense of identity and purpose. Both Aristotle's practical wisdom and Ignatian discernment involve emotional engagement. A balanced emotional sensitivity is a vital part of good decision-making. Hence, Ignatius teaches that we must attend to our desires as the basis for true discernment.

How is desire to be shaped? Aristotle suggests that we can train our emotional responses by undertaking appropriate actions, even when initially we do not feel inclined. This closely resembles Ignatius's teaching in the *Spiritual Exercises* about what he calls *agere contra*—that is, literally "to go against" those instincts that are self-serving rather than directed to-

---

9. Aristotle, *Nicomachaean Ethics*; see Gerard J. Hughes, *Aristotle on Ethics* (London: Routledge, 2001), 179.

wards the good of others. Such instincts are what Ignatius calls "disordered attachments," and they indicate a lack of spiritual freedom.

The notion of "going against" self-serving instincts appears at the beginning of the Second Week in the key contemplation called "The Call of the King" (Exx 97). Our response to Christ's call demands that Christian disciples go "against their sensuality and their carnal and worldly love"—that is, an obsession with material satisfaction, status, or power. It is clear that, for Ignatius, "going against" is not simply a question of willpower. For Ignatius, we also need "the grace"—that is, God's empowerment.

Discernment also became a key value in early Christian spirituality. How are we to lead a spiritual life? The important value was "balance," for which discernment was the guiding principle. As Antony of Egypt asserted, "Some wear out their bodies by fasting, but because they have no discernment, this only puts them further away from God."[10] Importantly, among the signs of true discernment in desert spirituality are the social virtues of compassion, charity, and attentiveness to other people. John Cassian's spiritual *Conferences*, based partly on his experience of desert monasticism, preached moderation or balance as the virtue that measures everything else and avoids the excesses of other deceptively spiritual values. In Cassian, discernment is also related to cultivating wisdom for the benefit of the community.[11] In later centuries, the great theologian Thomas Aquinas's teaching on discernment (based partly on Aristotle) is again connected to the virtue of "practical prudence." Discernment regulates all other virtues.

10. See Benedicta Ward, ed., *The Desert Fathers: Sayings of the Early Christian Monks* (London: Penguin Books, 2003), chapter 10, "Discretion," 88, no. 1.

11. See Colm Luidheid, ed., *John Cassian: Conferences* (Mahwah, NJ: Paulist Press, 1985).

Ignatian spirituality summarizes this longer discernment tradition. At the beginning of the *Spiritual Exercises*, in the Principle and Foundation (Exx 23), the basis of discernment is freedom from what Ignatius calls "disordered attachments" so that we are able to judge and to choose in the light of our true purpose. Ignatius understood well that the purpose of life is to shape our characters so that we are able to live productively and at peace with ourselves and with other people. For this to be the case, everyone is called to make difficult choices on a daily basis. These will concern the things we use, the people we associate with, the values we embrace, the projects we take on, and the attitudes which direct our thinking, judging, and decisions.

Within the dynamic of the *Spiritual Exercises*, the gift of discernment becomes the means by which we come to know ourselves truly and to recognize the movement of God's Spirit in our lives. First, we reflect on our own life. Then, a contemplative cultivation of spiritual insight leads to the ability to distinguish between good and bad influences, resulting in a growing capacity to maintain a balanced life. Thus, discernment is based on a contemplative attentiveness to God. The ability to choose wisely grows out of contemplation of Jesus' life in the Gospels and through the daily practice of spiritual attentiveness, already mentioned, known as the Examen.

Ignatius slowly learned this contemplative approach to making good decisions through his own profound inner struggles with God and with himself. Crucially, Ignatius teaches us to attend to our desires as the basis for discernment. For Ignatius, spiritual "consolation" involves what he calls "the good spirit" guiding us via life-enhancing desires rather than through superficial "wants." Thus, according to Ignatius, true consolation, while profoundly challenging, involves an increase of love for God as well as a deepening of our human love, an increase of hope and faith, an interior joy, an attraction towards the spiritual, and a deep tranquility and peace.

Throughout the *Spiritual Exercises*, Ignatius returns again and again to the subject of desire, which is always directed towards a deep way of living and of making choices. For Ignatius, the spiritual journey is basically away from fragmentation toward harmony and away from the surface of life to the deep center of our true selves and of life's true meaning.

DISCERNMENT: INDIVIDUAL OR SOCIAL?

Ignatian "discernment of spirits" is frequently understood purely in terms of individual interiority, but this misses the point. The great Ignatian scholar Hugo Rahner is clear that Ignatian discernment involves our growing ability, through contemplation, to respond to everyday life with the mind and heart of Christ.[12] What does this imply? In the First Letter to the Corinthians, Paul makes it clear that having the mind of Christ—and living in "the Body of Christ"—involves a commitment to mutual enhancement beyond mere personal satisfaction. Interestingly, Pope Pius XI's 1931 encyclical *Quadragesimo Anno*, which helped shape Catholic social teaching and which appeared at a time of acute economic and political turmoil in Europe, explicitly highlights the Ignatian Exercises as "a most precious means of personal and social reform" and as a tool for the renewal of society.

Ignatius's teaching on discernment is radically self-forgetting. True spiritual wisdom, as well as choosing well, is embodied in service of our neighbor—the exemplar of which may be, as in the Good Samaritan parable (Luke 10:29-37), a despised outsider. The "Contemplation on the Incarnation" at the beginning of the Second Week of the *Spiritual Exercises* (Exx 101-9) invites us to contemplate the Trinity as the starting point for seeing and understanding human life and "the world" through God's own compassionate eyes.

Two other key meditations of the "Second Week" have powerful social implications. For example, the issue of discernment

---

12. Hugo Rahner, *Ignatius the Theologian* (San Francisco: Ignatius Press, 1990), 146, 154.

as presented in the meditation on the "Two Standards" (Exx 136–48) is not to choose between what is obviously good and what is obviously evil but between what initially merely appears to be good in the abstract and what is truly good in the actual circumstances of life. Ignatius highlights two very different ways of working for the kingdom of God—the way of power or the way of love. Christians face a temptation to use seemingly good things such as wealth and power to follow Jesus and to serve others. However, the ultimate word spoken by Jesus is that of vulnerable and risky service rendered only out of love. Those who wish to follow Jesus must choose the way of love and of "humility" that risks suffering and the cross.

Another meditation, on "Three Kinds of Humility" (Exx 165–68), is part of the preparation for what Ignatius calls "an election"—that is, choosing a way of life that is single-heartedly concerned with what he calls "the purpose for which I am created" (that is, who I truly am) and with "desiring to serve God" (that is, my sense of ultimate purpose). In modern understandings, "being humble" is not always positive because it seems to imply either something false or something self-demeaning. However, for Ignatius "humility" is the opposite of the prevailing sin of his own aristocratic class. This was *hidalguía*, that is, "pride" in being "the son of a somebody," having an inherited status and therefore dismissing other people as insignificant. In the end, humility means taking on the mind and heart of Jesus Christ. Interestingly, Ignatius describes the third way of being humble as "the most perfect." This way or level of humility moves us beyond mere duty. Here, our desire is simply to imitate Jesus Christ, who came to serve others rather than to be served.

MICHEL DE CERTEAU AND IGNATIAN MYSTICISM

Interestingly, the twentieth-century French Jesuit writer Michel de Certeau (1925–1986) offers some interesting concluding insights on Ignatian mysticism. De Certeau was an outstanding and creative multidisciplinary thinker. He was a historian (not least of spirituality and mysticism), a philosopher, and a social scientist. He wrote a volume of essays on social-scientific studies called *The Practice of Everyday Life* and coauthored a second. Throughout *The Practice of Everyday Life*, the Ignatian focus on finding God in our everyday practices is implicitly echoed in de Certeau's attention to the everyday tactics of ordinary people on the street. De Certeau's approach to everyday practices is value driven. In describing everyday life, its practices, and "ways of proceeding," he was not making a detached social scientific observation. Rather, he sought to inspire his readers, in the spirit of the Ignatian daily Examen, "to uncover for themselves, in their own situation, their own tactics (a struggle for life), their own creations (an aesthetic) and their own initiatives (an ethic)."[13]

De Certeau wrote that "daily life is scattered with marvels," and his reading of "the everyday" has a transfigured, even mystical, quality. His main collaborator, the French social scientist Luce Giard, is clear that de Certeau was predisposed to discern wonder in the everyday world by the Ignatian Spiritual Exercises. She suggests that *The Practice of Everyday Life* discloses daily life as mystical.[14] The foundations of de Certeau's book lie in his understanding of discernment in relationship to the Ignatian theme of "finding God in all things."

As we saw earlier, the key to "finding God in all things" is the "Contemplation for Attaining Love" at the end of the Spiritual Exercises (Exx 230–37). This expresses our desire for an all-embracing realization of, and response to, God present in all things as we move through our everyday world.

13. Michel de Certeau, *The Practice of Everyday Life*, vol. 1 (Berkeley: University of California Press, 1988), ix.

14. Luce Giard, "Introduction to Volume 1: History of a Research Project," in Michel de Certeau, Luce Giard, and Pierre Mayol, *The Practice of Everyday Life*, vol. 2 (Minneapolis: University of Minnesota Press, 1998), xiii–xxxiii. See also Luce Giard, "The Question of Believing," *New Blackfriars*, Special Issue on Michel de Certeau, 77, no. 909 (November 1996): 478.

> Here [what I desire] will be to ask for interior knowledge
> of all the great good I have received, in order that, stirred
> to profound gratitude, I may become able to love and
> serve the Divine Majesty in all things. (Exx 233)

Earlier in his life, Michel de Certeau wrote a groundbreaking article on the "Contemplation for Attaining Love (or Contemplation on the Love of God)".[15] There, he described Ignatian discernment as a movement from prayerful contemplation to a "spiritual reading" of the everyday world. This process was what de Certeau memorably called the Ignatian "mysticism of practice."

MARY WARD

As an appendix to Ignatian mysticism, I want to mention Mary Ward (1585–1645). Mary Ward was an English woman, born into a recusant Catholic family in Yorkshire, who eventually became a nun and inspired the foundation of two important groups of religious sisters dedicated to the education of young women. Mary Ward's spiritual values were profoundly influenced by the Ignatian Exercises.

It seems that Mary Ward had an early visionary experience that directed her toward religious life. Initially, she entered a Poor Clare monastery in northern France. However, with a band of companions, Mary Ward moved on to begin a community dedicated to a mission-oriented ideal rather than to austere monasticism. This seems to have been provoked by a "revelation" from God in 1609. Mary Ward then received a mystical direction from God in 1611 to "take the same of the

---

15. Michel de Cereau, "L'universalisme ignatien, mystique et mission," *Christus* 13, no. 50 (1966): 173–83.

Society," that is, the Jesuits.[16] Indeed, her plan or *Institutum* of 1621 expressed the same goals and the same structures as the Society of Jesus. My point is that behind Mary Ward's creation of a mission-oriented community of women, there were explicitly mystical elements.

The community has had a complicated history—not least because of critical reactions by male clerical Church authorities in its early days. However, it has survived to the present day. During the twentieth century, the main community was known as the Institute of the Blessed Virgin Mary (IBVM). However, in 2002 the community was finally allowed to adopt the Constitutions of the Society of Jesus and, also, to take Mary Ward's preferred name, the Congregation of Jesus, which echoes the official title of the Jesuits, the Society of Jesus.

Dag Hammarskjöld

Turning to the twentieth century, a particularly interesting example in relation to a mysticism of everyday practice is Dag Hammarskjöld (1905–1961), the Swedish economist (including a doctorate from Stockholm University) and diplomat. Originally a banker and then a senior Swedish civil servant, Hammarskjöld is best known as the second secretary general of the United Nations, from his appointment in 1953 until his death in an unexplained air crash in what is now Zambia on his way to negotiate a ceasefire in the Congo. Uniquely, he was posthumously awarded the Nobel Peace Prize.

Dag Hammarskjöld is considered to have been one of the most outstanding heads of the United Nations. This judgment relates not only to his work in strengthening the relatively new organization and to his diplomatic skills but to his exceptional personality. He was a deeply spiritual person who, among other

16. This is recorded in the Bar Convent Archives in York, B5 Letter 416 to Mgr Albergati 1620.

things, organized a meditation room in the UN headquarters in New York and kept a reflective diary from his youth until his death. This was eventually published as the famous book entitled *Markings* in its English version, with a foreword by his friend and famous English poet, W. H. Auden.[17]

In a 1953 radio interview shortly after his appointment as secretary general of the United Nations, Hammarskjöld offered a deep insight into the way he had been influenced in his approach to public service by mystical writings.

> The explanation of how man should live a life of active social service in full harmony with himself as a member of the community of spirit, I found in the writings of those great medieval mystics for whom "self-surrender" had been the way of self-realization, and who in single-ness of mind and inwardness had found strength to say yes to every demand which the needs of their neighbors made them face.[18]

The mystical writings he referred to were those by the Rhineland mystic Meister Eckhart and the Flemish theologian Jan Ruusbroec. In his foreword to *Markings*, W. H. Auden was clear that in Hammarskjöld the spiritual journey was intimately linked to the world of everyday action.

Hammarskjöld's diary, *Markings*, embraced an intimate revelation of the deep spiritual struggles that went along-side his active life, including eventually his responsibilities for promoting world peace as United Nations secretary general. There are many powerful and beautiful entries in the diary from an early age which reflect what I think of as his mystical sensibilities.

17. Dag Hammarskjöld, *Markings*, trans. W. H. Auden and Leif Sjöberg (London: Faber, 1966).

18. Quoted in Henry Van Dusen, *Dag Hammarskjöld: A Biographical Interpretation of Markings* (London: Faber, 1967), 47.

I am being driven forward
Into an unknown land.
The pass grows steeper,
The air colder and sharper.
A wind from my unknown goal
Stirs the strings
Of expectation.

Still the question:
Shall I ever get there?
There where life resounds,
A clear pure note
In the silence.[19]

Hammarskjöld came to a point where his life was subordinated to something greater: "Not I, but God in me."[20] *Markings* opens with a quotation from the mystic Meister Eckhart and, overall, the diary reveals numerous quotations from Eckhart as well as one from John of the Cross. While Hammarskjöld was culturally a Lutheran Christian, he was unconventional for a person of his time. Thus, he was happy to quote the Sufi mystic Rumi: "The lovers of God have no religion but God alone."[21]

MYSTICISM AND SOCIAL PRACTICE IN OTHER RELIGIONS

Finally, I want to conclude with a brief overview of the connections between mysticism and social practice in religions other than Christianity.

First, I will begin with the two other Abrahamic religions, Judaism and Islam. In Jewish mystical traditions, the connections

19. Hammarskjöld, *Markings*, 31.
20. Hammarskjöld, 87.
21. Hammarskjöld, 95.

with ethics are fairly explicit. For example, in orthodox Kabbalah, the starting point is the Torah. This is at the same time the Pentateuch or first five books of the Jewish Bible and "the Law." As a broad remark, a key ethical teaching present in the Law is hospitality to "the stranger"—a value that was later inherited by Christianity. Kabbalists also outline an immanent dimension to God alongside the divine "otherness." This dimension is God's interaction with humanity and with the cosmos. This interaction is through the medium of the *sephirot*—emanations or "attributes" of the divine. These are used by God as the means of persistently improving the human condition and of provoking human society to ethical behavior, not least assisting our fellow humans. In terms of the ethical dimension of Jewish mysticism, it is worth underlining that ethical practices are not only a question of morally right or wrong actions but are closely allied to the central idea of "virtue." This concerns the important characteristics and values associated with "being Jewish." Typically, such virtues include justice, truth-telling, peace, kindness, compassion, and self-respect balanced by respect for other people. Thus, our daily activity and all our human relations are potentially the medium for a spiritual, even mystical, interaction with God. In this way even the humble everyday Jew could attain to the mystical state of *devekut* or inner "cleaving" to God.[22]

As a general remark, Islam, rather like Judaism, focuses most strongly on what may be called an everyday model of spirituality. Islam is seen as a complete religious and social system embracing the whole of life rather than merely the performance of explicitly spiritual or ritual practices. There is no distinction between the sacred and secular dimensions of our

22. For an authoritative study of Jewish spiritual traditions, see Arthur Green, ed., *Jewish Spirituality*, 2 vols. (New York: Crossroad, 1987).

existence.[23] In that sense, the most famous mystical form of Islamic spirituality, Sufism, is fundamentally the internalization of the common life of Islam by connecting with its inner core.

I will now turn briefly to the Eastern spiritualities of Hinduism and Buddhism. Hinduism is often characterized as not merely a complete way of life but also as *sadhana*—a way or process that leads towards self-realization and spiritual freedom. A prominent feature of Hindu spirituality is the desire to move from what *presents* itself as real to the discovery of what is truly real. A fundamental notion is the call to live in the world while learning to be "world-less." This involves treating contingent reality as a transitory means to integration, and this demands a progressive loss of ego. The most widely read Hindu scripture is probably the Bhagavad Gita, a mystical text based on conversations between Prince Arjuna and the divine Krishna. Effectively, it is a practical manual on how to live well. Krishna's advice is to cultivate detachment while interacting with the world in order to devote all our work to the eternal spirit Brahman. During the nineteenth century, Ramakrishna (1836–1886) was a noted Hindu teacher and a famous mystic. Initiated into the Tantra tradition, Ramakrishna's teachings distinguished between the dark side of the everyday world, not least self-centered passions and actions, and higher forces such as selfless action, spiritual virtue, and love.[24]

Finally, Buddhism originated in India during the Fourth Century BCE with the person of Siddartha Gautuma. He renounced his wealthy background and sought a spiritual path that focused on the problem of human suffering. Siddartha eventually became known as the "enlightened one"

23. For a comprehensive collection of essays on spirituality in Islam, see Seyyed Hossein Nasr, ed., *Islamic Spirituality*, 2 vols. (New York: Crossroad, 1991).

24. See e.g., Arvind Sharma, *A Guide to Hindu Spirituality* (Bloomington, IN: World Wisdom, 2006).

or the "Buddha." The Buddha's teachings were intended to be a recipe for becoming free from the suffering of material existence, to escape the otherwise inevitable cycle of birth and rebirth (*samsara*), and ultimately to achieve liberation and enlightenment (*nirvana*). "Enlightenment" implies that we eventually overcome ignorance or the ways in which we misunderstand the true nature of existence. "Existence" has three characteristics. The first mark of existence is "Impermanence." Everything in the everyday world is contingent and contextual and therefore impermanent. Our mistake is to become attached to the everyday which results in "Suffering," the second mark of everyday existence. This implies a state of dissatisfaction or frustration. Finally, the third mark of existence is "No self." In other words, a true understanding of everyday reality leads us to realize that nothing, including ourselves, has an independent "self." *Nirvana*, final enlightenment and liberation, involves the ultimate extinction of suffering as we embrace our true nature in the absence of all separate identity. The conceptual framework of Buddhist teaching is known as the Four Noble Truths, the fourth of which is a Noble Eightfold Path for the spiritual journey. This includes abstaining from unethical behavior in speech, action, and living.[25]

25. For an overview of Buddhist spirituality, see Philip Sheldrake, *Spirituality: A Guide for the Perplexed* (London: Bloomsbury, 2014). See also Takeuchi Yoshinori, ed., *Buddhist Spirituality: Indian, Southeast Asian, Tibetan, Early Chinese* (New York: Crossroad, 1995), and also his *Buddhist Spirituality: Later China, Korea, Japan, and the Modern World* (New York: Crossroad, 1999).

CHAPTER SEVEN

THE MYSTIC AS
RADICAL PROPHET

My final chapter focuses on the theme of mystics as radical prophets. The basis for this theme is my belief that, in some people, there is a profound connection between their mystical journeys and their commitments to the promotion of social transformation and social justice. Unfortunately, some contemporary post-Christian proponents of the "new mysticism," as well as some Christian theologians who are critical of a contemporary drift to mysticism, suggest that "the mystical" has no role in public and political life.[1] I disagree profoundly with this view. For one thing, the most substantial representatives of the Christian mystical tradition opposed any notion of a purely privatized spiritual experience.

In a more specific sense, are there ways in which mysticism can be thought of as concerned with the world of politics? Echoing the outstanding French Jesuit writer on mysticism, Michel de Certeau, the contemporary American Catholic

---

1. E.g., Nicholas Lash, "The Church in the State We're In," in *Spirituality and Social Embodiment*, ed. L. Gregory Jones and James J. Buckley (Oxford: Blackwell, 1997), 126.

theologian David Tracy suggests that mystics, like the mad, represent a kind of "otherness" on the social margins. This "otherness" has the capacity to challenge traditional centers of power and privilege.[2] Because the way of "knowing" expressed in mystical texts is based on union with God rather than on the power of our human intellects to control reality, it bears some resemblance to the "subjugated knowledges" spoken of by the French postmodern philosopher Michel Foucault. This resists dominant structures of power and knowledge and opposes established forms of discourse rather than simply offering an attractive alternative.[3]

In this chapter, I will explore a number of examples of connections between mysticism and a radical approach to social engagement. For example, the medieval Flemish writer Jan van Ruusbroec believed in an essential connection between contemplation, ethics, and charity. In twentieth-century Christianity, one of the most striking examples is the German pastor and theologian Dietrich Bonhoeffer, who was murdered by the Nazis. Bonhoeffer was described as a mystic in the writings of the famous German theologian Jürgen Moltmann. Later in the twentieth century, the African American theologian Howard Thurman is sometimes described as a mystic because of his intense awareness of the unity of all people and of all reality. Howard Thurman was a major influence on Martin Luther King Jr. and on the Civil Rights Movement in the United States. The German Protestant liberation theologian and political activist Dorothee Sölle was also deeply inspired by Christian mysticism and believed that mystical consciousness and the mystical path were the sources both of spiritual healing and of true social resistance. A similar connection between contemplation and social liberation appears in the writings of

2. David Tracy, *On Naming the Present: God, Hermeneutics, and the Church* (Maryknoll, NY: Orbis Books, 1994), 3–6.

3. Michel Foucault, *Power/Knowledge: Selected Interviews and Other Writings 1972–77*, ET (London: Pantheon, 1980), 81.

the important Latin American liberation theologians Segundo Galilea, Leonardo Boff, and Gustavo Gutiérrez.

This chapter will end by briefly outlining some examples from other world religions such as the Jewish mystical Kabbalah, the nineteenth-century Hindu guru Sri Ramakrishna and his pupil Swami Vivekananda, and the Engaged Buddhism of the Vietnamese Buddhist monk Thich Nhat Hanh.

Jan van Ruusbroec—Mysticism, Charity, and Ethics

My first example is Jan van Ruusbroec, the fourteenth-century Flemish priest and theologian. He conceived of mysticism in terms of what he referred to as "the life common to all." This common life joined human beings to each other and also made everyday action and deep contemplation into a single whole. So, for Ruusbroec, the "spiritually elevated" person never ceases to be the "common" person. The elevated person "owes himself to all those who seek his help" and seeks to share "the life common to all" that is God's own life within us.[4] Ruusbroec was clear that the mystical life born of contemplation did not separate the mystic from other people but, on the contrary, connected human beings with one another in the service of all.

Ruusbroec understood that the highest state of the spiritual life was expressed by the community-minded person who wished above all to share with everyone else what she or he had received spiritually. In that sense, Ruusbroec questioned a detached approach to the contemplative life and rejected the common medieval interpretation of the story of Martha and Mary in the Gospel of Luke, chapter 19. This was usually described in terms of a clear distinction between a

4. For Ruusbroec's mystical writings, see James Wiseman, ed., *John Ruusbroec: The Spiritual Espousals and Other Work* (Mahwah, NJ: Paulist Press, 1985). All quotations are from this translated edition.

lower, everyday active life and a higher, contemplative life.
In a human life that is truly at one with God, contemplative
union and self-giving action alternate in a way that transgresses
the boundary between interiority and everyday existence. According to Ruusbroec, this way of life is truly at one with the
rhythm of the inner life of the God-as-Trinity.

In one of Ruusbroec's mystical works, *The Sparkling Stone*,
he affirms:

> A person who has been sent down by God from these
> heights is full of truth and rich in all the virtues. . . .
> He will therefore always flow forth to all who need him,
> for the living spring of the Holy Spirit is so rich that it
> can never be drained dry. . . . He therefore leads a com-
> mon life, for he is equally ready for contemplation or for
> action and is perfect in both.[5]

Elsewhere, Ruusbroec writes:

> Thus this man is just, and he goes towards God by inward
> love, in eternal work, and he goes in God by his fruitive
> inclination in eternal rest. And he dwells in God; and yet
> he goes out towards all creatures, in a spirit of love to-
> wards all things, in virtue and in works of righteousness.
> And this is the supreme summit of the inner life.[6]

Ruusbroec was quite clear that those people who practice the
attainment of a peaceful inwardness as the goal of their prayer
and disregard charity or ethics are, of all people, most guilty
of spiritual wickedness.[7]

---

5. Ruusbroec, *The Sparkling Stone*, ET in Wiseman, ed., *Spiritual Espousals*, 184.
6. Wiseman, ed., *Spiritual Espousals*, Book 1, part 2, chapter LXV.
7. Wiseman, ed., *Spiritual Espousals*, Book II, "The Interior Life," 136–43.

In her classic work *Mysticism*, Evelyn Underhill described Ruusbroec as one of the greatest Western Christian mystics precisely because Underhill believed that selfless service of others was a major characteristic of all genuine Christian mysticism and marked it out from mysticism in other world religions. While we would question Underhill's final judgment about other religions, I believe she is correct in her observation about the heart of Christian mysticism.[8] This corresponds to my own perception over many years that the greatest contemplative figures in Western spiritual traditions were also people of immense pastoral and prophetic energy. They moved naturally from a deep encounter with God to an engagement with the outer world to which our God was irrevocably committed.

Jürgen Moltmann—and Dietrich Bonhoeffer

Moving forward to the twentieth century, Jürgen Moltmann is a German Protestant theologian and one of the most widely read theologians of the second half of the century. He was formerly Professor of Systematic Theology at the University of Tübingen. Moltmann lived through the Nazi period and the horrors of World War II. He was captured by the British in early 1945 and moved to a POW camp in Scotland. He was repatriated to Germany in April 1948.

This painful experience led Moltmann from a purely notional Christianity to a deeper experience of God—the presence of God in a personal "dark night" of the spirit. This experience left him with a longing which impelled him towards hope. He suggested that God found him rather than that he found God.

---

8. See Evelyn Underhill, *Mysticism: The Nature and Development of Spiritual Consciousness* (Oxford: One World Publications, 1993).

In his short (and often overlooked) book *Experiences of God*, Moltmann writes of the necessarily ethical dimension of the mystical *sapientia experimentalis* (experiential wisdom).[9] This concept is close to Martin Luther's own understanding of spirituality and to Paul Tillich's related concept of "participative knowledge." However, the most interesting aspect of Moltmann's approach to mysticism is his outline of a fivefold process to replace the more traditional patristic-medieval *triplex via* or "threefold way." This process is really a continuous circular movement rather than a succession of separate spiritual stages. It begins with our ongoing social engagement with the ambiguities and pains of the external, everyday world. For example, the initial and instinctive human response to social injustice is to want to change things. This action for change inevitably leads to a realization that a truly Christian response to social injustice has to be supported by contemplation. Contemplation, which in Moltmann's terms is focused on the story of Jesus Christ in the Gospels, leads to a movement away from self and from false images of God toward "God alone." Our encounter with the living God, purified of selfishness, is what has been classically described in Western approaches to mysticism as "union." However, this union is not an end in itself. The purpose of mystical union is not to remain in a pure and detached spiritual state aside from our responsibilities in everyday life. What we encounter at the heart of God is the cross. Union with God, therefore, leads to a deeper identification with the person of Jesus, who moved out of himself in kenotic, self-giving love. Thus, the mystical journey leads the Christian believer back from union with God, which now becomes a new point of departure, to the practice of everyday discipleship and social engagement. This is the true meaning of ecstasy, *ekstasis*. Ecstasy is not simply

9. Jürgen Moltmann, "The Theology of Mystical Experience," in his *Experiences of God* (Philadelphia: Fortress Press, 1980), 55–80.

some emotional or visionary experience. It is to step out from oneself in self-giving love.

> As long as we do not think that dying with Christ spiritually is a substitute for dying with him in reality, mysticism does not mean estrangement from action; it is a preparation for public, political discipleship.[10]

Thus, Moltmann implies that in the person of someone like Dietrich Bonhoeffer (1906–1945), one of his heroes, who was executed by the Nazis, the mystic may also be a martyr. For Moltmann, the icon of mysticism therefore becomes the political martyr as much as the contemplative monk. In the words of Moltmann:

> The place of mystical experience is in very truth the cell—the prison cell. The "witness to the truth of Christ" is despised, scoffed at, persecuted, dishonored and rejected. In his own fate he experiences the fate of Christ. His fate conforms to Christ's fate. That is what the mystics called *conformitas crucis*, the conformity of the cross. . . . Eckhart's remark that suffering is the shortest way to the birth of God in the soul applies, not to any imagined suffering, but to the very real sufferings endured by "the witness to the truth."[11]

Interestingly, Moltmann notes that Dietrich Bonhoeffer prepared for the prison cell and for martyrdom by staying in a Benedictine monastery.

> Dietrich Bonhoeffer did this in the monastery at Ettal, before he was arrested and put in prison in Tegel. It is useful to learn to be alone and to be silent before we are condemned to these things. It is liberating to sink into

10. Moltmann, *Experiences of God*, 73.
11. Moltmann, 72.

the wounds of the risen Christ in meditation, so as to experience our own torments as his fate.[12]

In my own writings, I have suggested previously that Dietrich Bonhoeffer was a notable example of prophetic spirituality.[13]

HOWARD THURMAN

Another striking example of the mystic as radical prophet is the remarkable person Howard Thurman (1899–1981), the African American theologian who spent time later in life as dean of chapel at Boston University. Howard Thurman was a major influence on Martin Luther King Jr. and therefore on the American Civil Rights Movement in the 1950s and 1960s.

Thurman was a teacher of the "way of mysticism," where he spoke on behalf of the underprivileged. In his lectures "Mysticism and Social Change," Thurman wrote:

> It is not only the socialist but also the confirmed mystic or the man seeking the fullness of the vision of God who must say truly, "While there is a lower class, I am in it. While there is a criminal element, I am of it. While there is a man in jail, I am not free." The distinction between personal selfishness and social selfishness which we are wont to make, must forever remain artificial and unrealistic.[14]

During the period when Thurman was on the faculty of Howard University in Washington, DC, from 1932 to 1944, he and his wife were asked to be part of a delegation on a

---

12. Moltmann, 75.

13. Philip Sheldrake, *The Spiritual Way: Classic Traditions and Contemporary Practice*, (Collegeville, MN: Liturgical Press, 2019), 124–25.

14. Howard Thurman, "Mysticism and Social Change," *Eden Theological Seminary Bulletin* (Spring 1938), 28.

"Pilgrimage of Friendship" to India. As a representative of the USA's "minority group," the invitation to India reflected a belief that Thurman could make an important contribution in a country still under British imperial rule and divided by the caste system into groups of people who were either the acceptable "touchables" or the despised so-called "untouchables." While there, Thurman had a profound visionary religious experience in the Khyber Pass. This vision determined the direction of his social witness for the rest of his life.[15]

In his helpful book on the mysticism of Howard Thurman, Luther Smith Jr. suggests that Thurman's primary identity was as a mystic "who recognized the necessity of social activism for enabling and responding to religious experience."[16] In Thurman's own words:

> Therefore, the mystic's concern with the imperative of social action is not merely to improve the condition of society. . . . The basic consideration has to do with the removal of all that prevents God from coming to himself in the life of the individual.[17]

There is an important factor in Howard Thurman's mysticism which distinguishes it from some common understandings of mysticism as something entirely separate from everyday action and knowledge. Thurman's version of religious experience strongly affirms "knowing" the everyday world rather than moving beyond it. In other words, a vision of God gives

---

15. See Luther E. Smith Jr., *Howard Thurman: The Mystic as Prophet*, 3rd ed. (Richmond, IN: Friends United Press, 2007), 8. Luther E. Smith Jr. also edited the volume on Howard Thurman in the Orbis Books series Modern Spiritual Masters. See *Howard Thurman: Essential Writings* (Maryknoll, NY: Orbis Books, 2006).

16. Smith Jr., *Howard Thurman: The Mystic as Prophet*, 15.

17. In Thurman's Lawrence Lecture, "Mysticism and Social Action," First Unitarian Church of Berkeley, October 1978.

us a proper sense of the value of—and need for—a commitment to society, especially to fighting evil.[18]

For Thurman, as an expression of the fuller meaning of love, we seek to change the prevailing social order. In Thurman's own words, "In his effort to achieve the good [the mystic] finds that he must be responsive to human need by which he is surrounded."[19]

Chapter VI, "Prophetic Mysticism" in Luther Smith's study of Thurman's mysticism quotes Abraham Heschel, the famous Jewish theologian. Heschel suggested that the prophets of ancient Israel were shaped by intense encounters with God. Such profound experiences were more social than personal because the purpose of the prophets' messages was to communicate God's profound concern for the welfare of God's people.[20]

Thurman's prophetic mysticism expressed his deep concern for the sufferings of the oppressed (especially Black Americans) and his goal of a social order governed by an ethic of love. Thurman's mystical spirituality suggested a religious imperative to transform the political and social realities of his time and place.[21]

Thurman had a profound sense of hope. This hope was based on his sense of power and meaning which he received through his deep religious experience. The basis for hope in the midst of hate (for example, racial prejudice) was Thurman's mystical reliance on his encounter with God.[22]

DOROTHEE SÖLLE

Another significant figure in the second half of the twentieth century was Dorothee Sölle. She was a feminist thinker

18. See Smith Jr., *Howard Thurman*, 78–79.
19. Thurman, "Mysticism and Social Change," 30.
20. See Smith Jr., *Howard Thurman*, 195–96.
21. See Smith Jr., *Howard Thurman*, 205.
22. See Smith Jr., *Howard Thurman*, 214.

and a political activist, as well as being a significant German Protestant theologian. However, many people consider her not only to have been deeply influenced by Christian mysticism (for example, by the fourteenth-century mystical figures, the Beguine Marguerite Porete and the Dominican Meister Eckhart) but also to have been herself a mystic and a highly significant twentieth-century spiritual-political figure.

As Dorothee Sölle herself suggested,

> I am neither professionally anchored nor personally at home in the two institutions of religion—the church and academic theology. It is the mystical element that will not let go of me.[23]

Sölle's life and thought was profoundly shaped by the Nazi period. Her parents were strongly anti-Nazi and her father was partly Jewish. This background—as well as the painful questions provoked by the Nazi concentration camps about God and God's relationship with human suffering—shaped all of her work, whether her activism or her theology. Indeed, Sölle regularly asked herself and her readers whether theology was actually possible in the aftermath of Auschwitz. In this context, Sölle was profoundly influenced by the example of Dietrich Bonhoeffer (already mentioned)—both his desire to integrate politics and theology and his martyrdom as a Christian who opposed Nazi ideology and then paid the ultimate price.

In her book, *The Silent Cry: Mysticism and Resistance*, just quoted, Dorothee Sölle reveals how in mysticism, rather than in institutional Christianity, she found the kind of integration of inner spiritual experience and radical social action that she sought. Her book refers to a mysticism of "wide-open eyes." For Sölle, resistance to injustice in order to change the world must have mystical roots. This is expressed in another essay

23. See Dorothee Sölle, *The Silent Cry: Mysticism and Resistance*, ET (Minneapolis: Fortress Press, 2001), 1.

"To be Amazed, to Let Go, to Resist."[24] In her book *The Silent Cry*, part II, "Places of Mystical Experience," chapter 8 "Suffering" outlines one of her five "places" of mystical experience. For Sölle, mystics were people who sought to transmute the pain of human suffering into the birth of something new and life-giving. In this she was influenced by such mystics as Meister Eckhart, who taught that human suffering has meaning as a process of dying to oneself and also of becoming more open to God.

Interestingly, in her chapter 8, Sölle explicitly refers to and quotes from the book *On Job: God-Talk and the Suffering of the Innocent* by the Peruvian priest and liberation theologian Gustavo Gutiérrez.[25] Sölle had moved away from her background in conventional German Protestant theology toward both the mystical and the theme that "God is justice." She effectively became a European liberation theologian and saw the link between mysticism and a confrontation with collective human suffering as a major concern. Sölle found in Latin American liberation theology—and its option for the poor—a form of social mysticism that transcended the conventional categories of academic theology. Dorothee Sölle undertook extensive travels in Latin America where she befriended a number of liberation theologians, including Gustavo Gutiérrez, who shared her interest in spirituality and mysticism.

An important aspect of the relationship between mysticism and social engagement is in terms of the purification of our motivations and the resulting transformation of our social practice. For Dorothee Sölle, there are three dimensions or levels

24. See the English translation of Dorothee Sölle's "To be Amazed, to Let Go, to Resist: Outline for a Mystical Journey Today," in *Mysticism and Social Transformation*, ed. Janet Ruffing (Syracuse, NY: Syracuse University Press, 2001), 45–51.

25. For the English translation, see Gustavo Gutiérrez, *On Job: God-Talk and the Suffering of the Innocent* (Maryknoll, NY: Orbis Books, 1987).

of what she understood by "mystical consciousness."[26] First, there is what she called "amazement" or "being amazed." This concept is not merely wonder or praise of God but, in Sölle's words, is something that "tears the veil of triviality" because it is touched by the spirit of life. Without this reinspiration, nothing new begins. At this first level, we do not embark upon the path of our spiritual journey merely as aimless seekers but as people who have already been "found." By this Sölle meant that any effective action for social justice that we undertake is always preceded by the goodness of God that we have already experienced personally. Then, there is the second level of mystical consciousness, "leaving oneself" and letting go. As Sölle put it, this is a process of "missing God." The notion of "missing God" refers to a process of purification that comes about when we realize how distant we in fact are from leading a truly spiritual life and also from the deep reality of God. We therefore necessarily go through a process of "dis-education" (in her words). This involves a growth in freedom, especially in our contemporary Western culture, becoming free from what Sölle referred to as "the addictive and compulsive mechanisms of consuming." This disordered identification of a satisfactory life with consumerism can be summed up in an equation such as "I have, or I choose, and therefore I am"! Third and finally, there is the level of what Sölle called "a living in God." This is her version of the classical mystical concept of "union with God" or the *via unitiva*—the unitive way. This final level of mystical consciousness involves healing. Our healing is also the foundation of true resistance to social injustice. We only become capable of healing others and of healing the world to the extent that we ourselves have first been healed.

Dorothee Sölle was a constant and robust exponent of social justice who found in the experience of mysticism—that is, a

26. See her essay "To be Amazed, to Let Go, to Resist," in *Mysticism*, ed. Ruffing, 45–51.

real and deep encounter with God—the foundations of her ability to stand with the oppressed. This made her writings a unique synthesis of mystical spirituality and social justice.

THE MYSTICAL AND THE WAY OF LIBERATION

Turning explicitly to classic examples of liberation theology, a number of Latin American theological writers over the last fifty years or so have argued that the mystical-contemplative way is a necessary dimension of social engagement. Interestingly, the Spanish theologian Gaspar Martinez has suggested that what he calls "worldly theologies," those modern Roman Catholic theologies that engage explicitly with the public dimensions of life, are simultaneously the ones that focus most sharply on the mystery of God. They encourage a greater rather than a lesser emphasis on spirituality and mysticism.[27]

Because people referred to as political theologians or liberation theologians have been explicitly concerned with social engagement—indeed, with the prophetic role of Christianity in relation to social transformation—it is particularly instructive to note the degree to which the connections between contemplation or mysticism and social action are central to the writings of such theologians. I will now briefly outline the thinking of three important Latin American liberation theologians, the Chilean Segundo Galilea, the Brazilian Leonardo Boff, and the Peruvian Gustavo Gutiérrez.

SEGUNDO GALILEA (1928–2010)

Within the tradition of liberation theology, the Chilean theological writer Segundo Galilea wrote a significant amount concerning the mystical or the contemplative dimensions of

---

27. See Gaspar Martinez, *Confronting the Mystery of God: Political, Liberation and Public Theologies* (New York: Continuum, 2001).

political and social responses to injustice. Galilea suggested that there needs to be a movement away from the notion that an effective political response to social injustice can be purely ethical or structural. If our responses to poverty and injustice in the world are only structural, the new structures on their own may simply become new forms of oppression. We need to move towards the truly spiritual experience of discovering the compassion of God present in the poor as well as in Jesus Christ. According to Galilea, humans are not able to find true compassion or to create structures of deep transformation without entering contemplatively into Jesus' own compassion. Only contemplative-mystical practice, within a context of social action, is capable of bringing about the change of heart in us that is necessary for a lasting human solidarity—particularly a solidarity that is capable of embracing the oppressors in ways that challenge them as well as embracing the oppressed. Thus, according to Galilea, exterior social engagement must be accompanied by a process of radical interior transformation and liberation from self-seeking. This is the heart of what he refers to as "integral liberation."[28]

However, in this respect not all forms of contemplative practice are helpful. With his considerable knowledge of the Western mystical tradition, particularly of sixteenth-century Spanish mystical writings, Segundo Galilea was profoundly critical of a certain kind of Neoplatonic mysticism in Western Christianity.

> It has . . . a strongly transcendent orientation and ne-
> glects bodily, historical, temporal mediations. It tends to
> make of contemplation an ascent to God in which the
> temporal sphere is gradually left behind until an exclusive

28. Segundo Galilea, "The Spirituality of Liberation," *The Way: A Review of Christian Spirituality* (July 1985): 186–94.

absorption in God is reached. This tendency can easily become a form of escape.[29]

Galilea called for a reformulation of the idea of contemplation and of the mystical. He suggests that at the heart of the mystical tradition has always been the notion of contemplation as a supreme act of self-forgetfulness rather than a preoccupation with personal interiority. In the teachings of the great mystics, contemplation has always been related to the classic Christian themes of the cross and dying to oneself.

> This implies the crucifixion of egoism and the purification of the self as a condition of contemplation. This crucifixion of egoism in forgetfulness of self in the dialectic prayer-commitment will be brought to fulfilment both in the mystical dimension of communication with Jesus in the luminous night of faith, and also in the sacrifice which is assumed by commitment to the liberation of others. The "death" of mysticism and the "death" of the militant are the two dimensions of the call to accept the cross, as the condition of being a disciple.

> The desert as a political experience liberates [the Christian] from egoism and from the "system," and is a source of freedom and of an ability to liberate.[30]

LEONARDO BOFF

Another one of the most important writers on the interface of liberation theology and mysticism is the Brazilian theologian and former Franciscan priest, Leonardo Boff (born 1938). Boff has sharply criticized the traditional spiritual and

---

29. Segundo Galilea, "Liberation as an Encounter with Politics and Contemplation," ET in *Understanding Mysticism*, ed. Richard Woods (London: Athlone Press, 1981), 529–40; see 531.
30. Galilea, "Liberation as an Encounter," 535–36.

monastic formula of *ora et labora* (prayer and work) on the grounds that it promotes a kind of spiritual parallelism. At best, the word *et* has come to stand for a process of alternating interior prayer and exterior action in the everyday world. In classical approaches to Christian spirituality, contemplation was viewed as the source of all that had value. The practice of everyday life or action was not a direct mediation of God but was only of value to the extent that it was "fed" by contemplation. According to Boff, the whole conceptual framework implies a type of what he calls "spiritual monophysitism." That is, the unique nature of prayer redeems the creaturely and natural profaneness of work.[31] In some contemporary thinking, influenced by the dominance of social and political theory, this parallelism of prayer and work continues to exist but is reversed, as it were. That is, everyday practice rather than contemplation has been given priority so that contemplation becomes another, secondary, form of social practice. Against this viewpoint, Boff argues for an equal and mutually dependent relationship between prayer and work "treating them as two spaces that are open to one another and imply each other."[32] This mutual dependency produces a unity in what Boff refers to as the "mysticism-politics relationship."

Leonardo Boff coined a new phrase to describe being contemplative while engaged fully in the public spaces of radical political action—*contemplativus in liberatione*, that is, "contemplative in liberation." This echoes Ignatius Loyola's concept of *contemplativus in actione*, "contemplative in action." This unity of prayer and liberation is based on a living faith that, in Boff's words, "defines the 'from where' and the 'towards where' of our existence, which is God and his design

31. Leonardo Boff, "The Need for Political Saints: From a Spirituality of Liberation to the Practice of Liberation," ET in *Cross Currents* 30, no. 4 (Winter 1980/81): 369–84. See 371.

32. Boff, "Need for Political Saints," 373.

of love, that is communicated through, and materialized, in all things."[33] Thus, the contemplative and the mystical "is not carried out only in the sacred space of prayer, nor in the sacred precinct of the church; purified, sustained, and nurtured by living faith, it also finds its place in political and social practice."[34]

The most destructive things in human society arise from the variety of ideologies that claim to contain absolute truth, definitive ethical values, or a powerful mixture of both. In the end, the Christian mystical tradition does point to "truth," but to a truth that is not conclusive, on a way that is no way, in the direction of a somewhere that is beyond any definitive arrival. The point that the Christian mystical tradition makes is that what is most true cannot finally be captured either intellectually or emotionally.

GUSTAVO GUTIÉRREZ

Finally, the Peruvian theologian, Gustavo Gutiérrez, now a Dominican and a professor at the University of Notre Dame, Indiana, is one of the best-known, iconic figures in the tradition of liberation theology. His writings draw upon mystical thinking, especially the classic sixteenth-century figures, Teresa of Avila, John of the Cross, and Ignatius Loyola. Gutiérrez played a leading role as a theological advisor at the famous and important 1968 conference of Latin American bishops at Medellín. The conference translated the ideas and values of the Second Vatican Council into the Latin American context. Gutiérrez's seminal work, *A Theology of Liberation* (1971), set the tone for the development of liberation theology among a range of other people, both Roman Catholic and Protestant.[35] Another of his books, *We Drink from Our Own Wells: The*

33. Boff, 372.
34. Boff, 374.
35. Gustavo Gutiérrez, *A Theology of Liberation*, ET (Maryknoll, NY: Orbis Books, 1973).

Spiritual Journey of a People (1983), related his approach to liberation theology specifically to spirituality.[36] The book unequivocally affirms the inherently collective nature of human identity. It also underlines that spirituality, theology, and social action are profoundly connected to each other. For Gutiérrez, spirituality, not least its mystical aspects, is the source of all true theology. The heart of spirituality and mysticism is the practice of Christian discipleship. This practice of discipleship involves embracing "the other," especially the poor, who are the special focus of God's gratuitous love. This "preferential option" for the poor is a key aspect of the mystical-prophetic spirituality which lies at the heart of Gutiérrez's liberation theology. As he says, "Everything begins with silence; that is the first step in speaking of God; that is the moment of listening and prayer; later the language engendered in that quiet will come."[37] Interestingly, the title *We Drink from Our Own Wells* echoes the great medieval Cistercian mystical writer Bernard of Clairvaux and overall, as already noted, Gutiérrez draws explicitly upon the great sixteenth-century Spanish mystics.

In Gutiérrez's *On Job: God-Talk and the Suffering of the Innocent*,[38] the biblical figure of Job seeks an answer to his experience of innocent suffering. Job robustly confronts God face-to-face. In Gutiérrez's thinking, Job comes to realize that his suffering is not unique but is an example of the injustice suffered by "nonpersons," for example, the poor. Part III of the book is entitled "The Language of Contemplation." This underlines that, for Gutiérrez, silence and contemplative listening are the key to his theology of liberation. Job comes to realize that God's love cannot be reduced to human

36. Gustavo Gutiérrez, *We Drink from Our Own Wells: The Spiritual Journey of a People*, 20th ed., ET (Maryknoll, NY: Orbis Books, 2003).
37. Gutiérrez, *We Drink from Our Own Wells*, xviii.
38. Gustavo Gutiérrez, *On Job: God-Talk and the Suffering of the Innocent*, 11th ed., ET (Maryknoll, NY: Orbis Books, 1998).

definitions of justice. Job receives no answer to his logical questioning of God about his innocent suffering. The response he actually receives is much deeper and more powerful than a logical "answer." Job discovers in self-abandonment to God a decisive experience of receiving the power of God's utterly gratuitous love which is, in the end, unfathomable.

MYSTICISM AND SOCIAL TRANSFORMATION IN OTHER RELIGIONS

Finally, I want to outline briefly a few examples from other world religions of the connection between mysticism and social transformation. I will focus briefly on Judaism and on Hinduism, but then I will take Buddhism as my main example.

While it is fair to suggest that the connections between mysticism and social justice or social transformation have been explored most explicitly in Christian writings, a similar point of connection exists in other mystical traditions, at least implicitly. All of them in different ways seek to counter the human ego—the self-centeredness that lies not only behind our distance from God or the Absolute but also behind our damaging separation from human others. A few examples may illustrate this point.

In Jewish mystical traditions, the connections between mysticism and ethics are fairly explicit. For example, in orthodox Kabbalah, the starting point is the Torah. The Torah at the same time refers to the first five books of the Jewish Bible, the Pentateuch, and also to "the Law." As a broad remark, a key ethical teaching present in the Jewish Law is hospitality to "the stranger"—a value that was later inherited by Christianity. Kabbalists also outline an immanent dimension to God alongside the divine "otherness." This dimension is God's interaction with humanity and with the cosmos. This interaction is through the medium of the *sephirot*—the emanations or "attributes" of the divine. These are used by God as the means of persistently improving the human condition and of provoking human society to ethical behavior, not least of which is assisting our fellow human beings.[39]

As I noted at the start of this chapter, outside the family of Abrahamic religions, a striking example of the connection between mysticism and social action was the nineteenth-century Hindu guru and mystic Sri Ramakrishna and his pupil Swami Vivekananda. Both of them not only sought to break down the barriers between "the spiritual" and the everyday aspects of life but, more radically, taught that serving the poor and despised was also to serve God. Swami Vivekananda was involved in contesting British imperialism in India as well as combatting the prevailing social injustice of both widespread material poverty and of the Hindu caste system.

To outsiders, certain versions of Hinduism (for example, Advaita) may give the impression of pursuing a path of utter detachment from the everyday world which, in the end, is deemed to be of no significance. This is a one-sided interpretation. For example, the scriptures known as the Bhagavad Gita may be thought of as a mystical text, but it is also deeply ethical in its teachings about how humans should exist and behave in the existential world. While the spiritual ideal is calm, balance, and detachment from any particular results (or "success") of our daily activity, we should not abstain from action in the everyday world.[40]

A modern Hindu movement, the Ramakrishna Mission looks back to the nineteenth-century spiritual teacher Sri Ramakrishna, as well as to his disciple Swami Vivekananda. Both teachers are considered by many people to be mystics.[41] Following their teachings, the Ramakrishna Mission continues to

39. E.g., see Alan Unterman, ed., *The Kabbalistic Tradition* (London: Penguin, 2008).

40. See English translation by Laurie Patton, ed., *The Bhagavad Gita* (London: Penguin, 2008).

41. E.g., see Swami Vivekananda, *The Four Paths of Self-Realization*, 2nd ed. (Valley Cottage, NY: Discovery Publisher, 2017).

work actively for the benefit of the poor and for the overall improvement of society.

Finally, most people associate the Indian lawyer and nationalist Mahatma Gandhi with the successful nonviolent campaign against British imperial rule in India. However, some people would also point to the deep and even mystical religiosity which underpinned Gandhi's broader views on social justice, on social discrimination associated with the caste system, and on a quest for social equality.

I now want to end this section by focusing on Buddhism. An important Buddhist teaching is nonattachment. One implication of this Buddhist teaching and its deepening through meditative practice relates to the kind of presence we are in the everyday world. The more we focus on ourselves as individuals, in other words the more we are egocentric, the more we see other people or the wider world simply from our self-centered viewpoint. Cultivating what Buddhism refers to as the "no-self" in everyone removes the barriers between different people and ultimately shapes a properly shared human world.

In the collection of essays on *Mysticism and Social Transformation*, edited by Janet Ruffing, a Roman Catholic sister and Professor Emerita at Yale Divinity School, the main example of a non-Christian approach to the connection between mysticism and social justice is an essay on Buddhism.[42] The writer of this essay, Donald Rothberg, is himself a Buddhist. He suggests that Buddhism offers vital resources for the integration of mysticism and social transformation. The path of transformation that leads to the end of suffering and ignorance and to *nirvana* (a transcendent state) is commonly understood as a threefold training. This training replaces the repetitive human cycles of greed, hatred, and delusion with generosity, loving-

42. See Donald Rothberg, "Awakening for All Beings: Buddhism and Social Transformation," in *Mysticism and Social Transformation*, ed. Janet Ruffing (Syracuse, NY: Syracuse University Press, 2001), 161–78.

kindness, and wisdom. The training embraces ethical integrity in human action, meditative development of our mind and heart, and insight known as Engaged Buddhism and relates this explicitly to social transformation. The project of Engaged Buddhism questions any split between Buddhist practice and social-political involvement. Engaged Buddhism is especially associated with the Vietnamese Zen monk, teacher, activist, and influential writer Thich Nhat Hanh, who died on January 22, 2022. Thich Nhat Hanh was deeply troubled by the suffering caused in the Vietnam War, which lasted twenty years, from 1955 to 1975. He teaches that responding to human suffering is a critical dimension of deep spiritual practice. It is inherent to the Buddhist concept of "mindfulness" and to the practice of mindfulness meditation.

Engaged Buddhism has two main aspects. First of all, it brings Buddhism into contemporary everyday life in all its aspects, including social and political relationships. Secondly, socially engaged Buddhism suggests that Buddhist teachings and practices can be applied to large-scale social, political, and economic systems. Engaged Buddhism has a variety of forms in Asia and the West, for example, grassroots activism leading to political action and an orientation towards social service and involvement with issues of war and peace, power and authority. The main point of Engaged Buddhism is to underline strongly that spiritual transformation and social transformation are not separate things.

For some exponents of Engaged Buddhism, facing individual suffering requires going to its roots in the surrounding, dominant social structures. Thich Nhat Hanh suggests that true human happiness can never be purely an individual matter.[43] He also suggests that cultivating the project of integrating personal and social transformation is a mystical

43. See Thich Nhat Hanh, *Teachings on Love* (Berkeley, CA: Parallax, 1998).

path.[44] In his words, "Do not kill. Do not let others kill. Find whatever means possible to protect life and prevent war."[45] In the mind of Thich Nhat Hanh, the point is not simply that we should *work* for justice and peace (which on its own may simply reflect our anger with injustice) but that, in ourselves, we are to "be peace."

CONCLUSION

To suggest that mystics may be "radical prophets" and that mysticism may be related to social action feels counterintuitive to some people. The word "mysticism" is widely assumed to relate essentially to intense inner experiences and to seeking to transcend the everyday ordinary. However, in her famous book, *Mysticism*, the mid-twentieth-century British writer Evelyn Underhill believed that selfless service of others was a particular characteristic of Christian mystics. Indeed, she saw the connection between mysticism and outward action as fundamental to Christian mysticism. For this reason, Underhill described the fourteenth-century Flemish mystical writer Jan van Ruusbroec (or John Ruysbroeck) as arguably the greatest Christian mystic. He was clear that the mystical life, while strongly related to contemplation, did not separate the people we call mystics from other people but joined human beings to one another in the service of all. Ruusbroec argued that people who practiced contemplative inwardness while disregarding the demands of ethics and charity were guilty of spiritual wickedness.[46]

44. See Thich Nhat Hanh, *Being Peace* (Berkeley CA: Parallax, 1987), especially 85–102.

45. Nhat Hanh, *Being Peace*, 98.

46. See "The Spiritual Espousals" in ed. Wiseman, *Spiritual Espousals*. See also Underhill, *Mysticism*.

The connection between mysticism and prophetic social action, while not unique to Christianity, is certainly a particularly strikingly element in Christian mysticism. As we have already seen, a number of writers over the last half century have argued that the mystical way is a necessary part of an engagement with social justice rather than separate from it. Structural change is needed for justice to prevail, but it must be complemented by a truly spiritual experience of discovering the compassion of God revealed in the poor. Humans are not able to find true compassion on their own or to create structures of radical social change, without first entering through contemplation into God's own compassion. Only contemplative practice, allied to our social engagement, is capable of bringing about the change of heart within us that is necessary for a lasting solidarity with the poor. In other words, effective and prophetic social action must be based on inner transformation and being freed from self-seeking. As Segundo Galilea reminds us, at the heart of the Christian mystical tradition has always been the belief that true contemplation is also a process of self-forgetfulness rather than a preoccupation with intense spiritual experiences in isolation.[47]

47. See Segundo Galilea, "Liberation as an Encounter."

CONCLUSION

Mysticism has a subversive quality. This counters a post-Enlightenment emphasis on "knowledge"—even of God—as related to objectivity, intelligibility, and clear definitions. As we have already seen, the outstanding French Jesuit thinker, Michel de Certeau (1925–1986) wrote significantly about mysticism. He suggested that people whose lives or writings spoke of the "otherness" of an essentially mysterious God were outsiders to the "Modern" project.

> Unbeknownst even to some of its promoters, the creation of mental constructs . . . takes the place of attention to the advent of the Unpredictable. That is why the "true" mystics are particularly suspicious and critical of what passes for "presence." They defend the inaccessibility they confront.[1]

De Certeau himself sought to speak to a world where institutional Christianity was no longer a privileged "site" of definitive meaning. Its status as an exemplary form of human society had been overtaken by the secular state. All that was

---

1. Michel de Certeau, *The Mystic Fable*, vol. 1, ET (Chicago: University of Chicago Press, 1992), p. 5, but see the complete introduction, 1–26.

left, in de Certeau's view, was a process of following after the perpetually departing person of Jesus Christ. The Christian call is to wander, to journey with no security apart from the story of Jesus Christ that is to be lived out rather than objectively described. Thus, paradoxically, both Christian practice and mysticism become "non-places." That is, they are disruptive acts of resistance at the heart of all human systems and attempts at definitive statements about reality. Nowadays such resistance is as much against secular political and economic systems as against the declining structures of institutional religion.

De Certeau referred to the "mystic fable." Mysticism is a fable because it makes no claim of definitive truth. It offers a language without power. Yet paradoxically, that is its strength. It questions all definitive systems of meaning. Once again, Christian believers are nowadays called to become wanderers who are always on the move in answer to a call to follow the Divine, without the certainties of power, authority, or even secure identity. The Christian community carries the "fabled" story of the risen Jesus, based on the empty tomb, which subverts all our fixed places, across an insecure world towards the unnameable "place" that we call "God."

For Michel de Certeau, mysticism was bound up with desire. "Desire" is a key word in his writings—one that he shared with French postmodern philosophers such as Michel Foucault and Jacques Derrida but which also summarizes the heart of the Ignatian spiritual tradition to which de Certeau was so indebted. For both the mystic and the postmodern person, "desire" expresses a certain kind of drivenness, an intensity and movement ever onward, inspired by what is not definitively known, not fully possessed, not fixed or final.

> They are, she [Hadewijch, the Beguine mystic] said,
> "drunk with what they have not drunk": inebriation
> without drinking, inspiration from one knows not where,
> illumination without knowledge. They are drunk with

what they do not possess. Drunk with desire. Therefore, they may all bear the name given to the work of Angelus Silesius: *Wandersmann*, the "wanderer."[2]

In de Certeau's early work and research on "mysticism" or "mystics" (*la mystique*—his word for the study of the mystical life), he can be more or less credited with establishing that, as a distinct category associated with subjective religious experiences, "mysticism" originated in early seventeenth-century France. Although de Certeau admitted that the remote origins of "mysticism" in this subjective sense lay much earlier in the late thirteenth century, especially with Meister Eckhart and the Beguines, he believed that the key point in its formalization was between the mid-sixteenth century and the mid-seventeenth century.[3] This paradigmatic period of mysticism was embedded in the context of what de Certeau refers to as "a loss." The various movements and writings were born (to use de Certeau's words) "with the setting sun." This sunset referred to the gradual demise of the previously dominant Christian religious worldview.[4] De Certeau asserted that the "dark nights" expressed in various mystical texts refer not merely to interior, subjective states of spiritual loss and absence but also to the global situation of a decline of religious faith in Western culture.[5]

De Certeau's interest in sixteenth- and seventeenth-century mysticism arose from the parallels he perceived between this period and his own late twentieth-century world when conventional religious language, especially the words of Scripture, could no longer be spoken to believers in the old ways.

2. See de Certeau, *Mystic Fable*, 299.
3. See the essay "Mystic Speech," in Michel de Certeau, *Heterologies: Discourse on the Other*, ET (Minneapolis: University of Minnesota Press, 1995), 83.
4. De Certeau, "Mystic Speech," 80.
5. De Certeau, "Mystic Speech," 81.

The world was increasingly seen as opaque and unreadable. In response to this spiritual disenchantment, the people we refer to as mystics sought to invent a different kind of place, one that was not a fully formed place at all. As de Certeau says himself, this "is only the story of a journey" that is necessarily fragmented and ultimately defies conclusive investigation. In his somewhat opaque words, "it overpowers the inquiry with something resembling a laugh."[6] Mystical literature offers a way forward for whoever paradoxically "asks directions to get lost" and seeks "a way not to come back."[7]

The initial impression is that the writings of Michel de Certeau concerning mysticism make it not only culturally and religiously marginal but also privatize it. Indeed, it is precisely an act of withdrawal from social "space" that gives rise to definable "mystics" in the sense described by de Certeau. "A prophetic faith organized itself into a minority within the secularized state."[8] In de Certeau's words, any ambition by the Roman Catholic Church after the Council of Trent to "reconstitute a political and spiritual 'world' of grace" ultimately failed. However, while de Certeau describes the movement of Christian spirituality to the cultural margins and its redistribution among mystic groups using new kinds of discourse, his understanding of "mysticism" is always as a social rather than a purely private, interior reality. In fact, de Certeau differs from many other twentieth-century commentators on mysticism precisely by *not* stressing individual mystical experiences in isolation but treating them as social phenomena. Mysticism is social not merely passively (that is, by being a reflection of a particular historical context) but also actively in that it affects and transforms the world, even self-consciously in that the

6. De Certeau, *Mystic Fable*, 13.
7. De Certeau, 14.
8. De Certeau, 20.

major mystics set out to create new forms of religious language and new religious groups.⁹

While the overall location or "site" of mystic literature in this period should not be oversimplified, Michel de Certeau suggested that there were "privileged places" for the development of mystical insight and practice within certain social groups. These groups were those people with little or no power in the public world. De Certeau noted that mysticism seemed to be closely related to forms of instability or social disinheritance. Thus, the rise of mystic literature often reflects the decline of a society based on various ideologies of stability—social, economic, and religious.

As I have already noted, for de Certeau, Christians are called to wander, with no security apart from the story of Jesus Christ. This is to be "practiced" rather than simply asserted.¹⁰ This Christian practice is profoundly disruptive of all social systems. De Certeau characterized the whole Christian tradition, as well as specifically mystical withdrawal, as a "way of proceeding"—in other words, not as an institution but rather as a pilgrimage. Indeed, Christian spirituality must avoid the temptation to settle down into a new and definitive "place."

> The temptation of the "spiritual" is to constitute the act of difference as a site, to transform the conversion into an establishment, to replace the "poem" [of Christ] which states the hyperbole with the strength to make history or to be the truth which takes history's place, or, lastly, as in evangelical transfiguration (a metaphoric movement), to take the "vision" as a "tent" and the word as a new land. In its countless writings along many different trajectories, Christian spirituality offers a huge inventory of difference,

9. See de Certeau, introduction to *Mystic Fable*.
10. See Michel de Certeau, "The Weakness of Believing: From the Body to Writing, a Christian Transit," in *The Certeau Reader*, ed. Graham Ward (Oxford: Blackwell Publishers, 2000), 226.

and ceaselessly criticizes this trap; it has insisted particularly on the impossibility for the believer of stopping on the "moment" of the break—a practice, a departure, a work, an ecstasy—and of identifying faith with a site.[11]

For de Certeau, the primary symbol of discipleship is now an empty tomb.[12] "He is not here; for he has been raised, as he said . . . indeed he is going ahead of you to Galilee." (Matt 28:6-7). God in Jesus cannot be pinned down to any moment or place. The "place" of Jesus is now perpetually elusive. He is always the one who has gone before us. De Certeau suggests that religious discourse is always in danger of being shattered. "Faith speaks prophetically of a Presence who is both immediately felt and yet still to come, who cannot be refused without a betrayal of all language, and yet who cannot be immediately grasped and held in terms of any particular language."[13]

At the end of Michel de Certeau's life, some people have suggested, his approach to spirituality eventually became somewhat detached from institutional religion and perhaps from conventional faith as it dispersed into the "practice of everyday life." However, we should remember that a "mysticism of practice" is a major characteristic of Ignatian spirituality. Spirituality is not so much the "ecstasy" of a religious mystic but a more tentative self-transcendence experienced in a succession of encounters with everyday "others." Yet the question remains. Is the enigmatic and poignant last page of the first volume of de Certeau's *The Mystic Fable* merely a nostalgic lament by a person who no longer has religious faith? Or was his "agnosticism" that of a person who (like the mystics he

11. Ward, *Certeau Reader*, 234.

12. Ward, 234.

13. Michel de Certeau, "Culture and Spiritual Experience," *Concilium* 19 (1966): 3–16.

revered) realizes that he cannot escape a never-ending journey of the human spirit beyond intellectual goals or spiritual
fulfilment? If, as seems more likely, a deep desire and faith
remained at the heart of de Certeau, the inner logic of his
thinking surely demanded that "the Divine Other" whom we
continually seek is necessarily beyond our limited language.

> He or she is a mystic who cannot stop walking and, with
> the certainty of what is lacking, knows of every place and
> object that it is *not that*; one cannot stay *there* nor be
> content with *that*. Desire creates an excess. Places are
> exceeded, passed, lost behind it. It makes one go further,
> elsewhere. It lives nowhere.[14]

Finally, as I asked previously in chapter 1, why is mysticism
so popular in our present times? I offered some thoughts at
that point. However, in summary, I think that there are also
two other closely related reasons. Both have to do with what
I see as the crises of our modern age and with the intense
human needs that result from this. First, many people want to
transcend the boundaries that characterize their normal worlds
and to experience unity with other people or harmony with
nature. They wish to overcome the divisions within humanity,
whether these are political, religious, social, or cultural. This
is because people experience these divisions as deeply destructive. As a result, people look for something "in common" on a
deeper spiritual level. However, because organized religion is
too often divided by mutual suspicion (as well as tarnished by
corruption and abuse), people look for spiritual contexts that
bypass these unattractive realities. Second, a variety of social,
economic, and political factors make many people dissatis-
fied with the ability of purely material enhancement to fulfill
human aspirations. Thus, the current crisis of meaning, fears

14. De Certeau, *Mystic Fable*, 299.

for the future of humanity and the environment, plus distaste with social and political corruption, may be transcended by accessing a level of consciousness that is available contemplatively rather than through purely material means. Mysticism therefore seems to offer a connection with the mysterious depths of human existence and of the cosmos.

The Contemplative-Mystical Way offers a sense of holism and of the interconnectedness of everyday life, as well as opening up a connection to "the more" and potentially to "the all." It is also a way of knowing beyond mere reason. It fosters attentiveness or what Buddhism would call "mindfulness." The Contemplative-Mystical Way also emphasizes being present in the fullest sense—and staying in place—rather than skipping around from one thing to another or simply dipping our toes into situations, events, and life. At the heart of being present is the cultivation of an immediacy of presence to the Absolute. Importantly, while in Christian understanding, the Absolute, God, offers love and healing, God also demands a generous response. This is to be shown by our own openhearted response to other people, not least to the stranger, and to the endangered world of wider creation. This mystical approach to "being present" and to a generosity of response also counters any tendency to treat "feeling good and happy" as an end in itself. The aim of the Contemplative-Mystical Way is to draw us beyond the immediate to the never-ending. It implies a transfiguration of the ordinary and being made one with the depths of ourselves, of other people, and of ultimate reality—that is, God. In this way, everyday reality is transfigured into something wondrous. As outlined earlier, for Michel de Certeau, the mystical way turns the spiritual seeker into a perpetual wanderer.

As we saw in chapter 6 and chapter 7, in the Christian mystical tradition there has been an important emphasis that contemplation should never be separated from ethical behavior (for example, in the medieval writings of John Ruusbroec).

More radically, the twentieth-century Chilean theologian Segundo Galilea wrote a great deal concerning the vital mystical or contemplative dimensions of responses to injustice. Social engagement must be accompanied by a process of interior transformation. This is the heart of what he called "integral liberation."[15] Galilea promoted a reformulation of the idea of contemplation and of the mystical. At the heart of the Christian tradition, he suggests, has always been the notion of contemplation as a supreme act of self-forgetfulness rather than a preoccupation with personal interiority. In the teachings of the great mystics, contemplation has always been related to the classic Christian theme of the cross.

> This implies the crucifixion of egoism and the purification of the self as a condition of contemplation. This crucifixion of egoism in forgetfulness of self in the dialectic prayer-commitment will be brought to fulfilment both in the mystical dimension of communication with Jesus in the luminous night of faith, and also in the sacrifice which is assumed by commitment to the liberation of others. The "death" of mysticism and the "death" of the militant are the two dimensions of the call to accept the cross, as the condition of being a disciple. . . . The desert as a political experience liberates [the Christian] from egoism and from the "system," and is a source of freedom and of an ability to liberate.[16]

---

15. Segundo Galilea, "The Spirituality of Liberation," *The Way: A Review of Christian Spirituality* (July 1985):186–94.

16. Galilea, "Liberation as an Encounter," 535–36.

SELECTED BIBLIOGRAPHY

Balthasar, Hans Urs von. *The Glory of the Lord: A Theological Aesthetics.* San Francisco: Ignatius Press, 1982–1989.

Bamberger, John E., ed. *Evagrius Ponticus: The Praktikos; Chapters on Prayer.* Collegeville, MN: Cistercian Publications, 1990.

Bouyer, Louis. "Mysticism: An Essay on the History of the Word." In *Understanding Mysticism*, edited by Richard Woods. London: Athlone Press, 1980.

Colledge, Edmund and James Walsh, eds. *Julian of Norwich: Showings.* Mahwah, NJ: Paulist Press, 1978.

Chryssavgis, John. *Light through Darkness: The Orthodox Tradition.* London: Darton, Longman & Todd, 2004.

Carmichael, Alexander, ed. *Carmina Gadelica.* Edinburgh: Oliver & Boyd, 1992.

The Cloud of Unknowing and Other Works. Edited by A. C. Spearing. London: Penguin, 2001.

The Cloud of Unknowing. Edited by James Walsh. Mahwah, NJ: Paulist Press, 1981.

De Certeau, Michel. *Heterologies: Discourse on the Other.* Minneapolis: University of Minnesota Press, 1995.

De Certeau, Michel. *The Mystic Fable*, vol. 1. Chicago: University of Chicago Press, 1992.

De Certeau, Michel. *The Practice of Everyday Life*, vol. 1. Berkeley: University of California Press, 1988.

De Certeau, Michel, Luce Giard, and Pierre Mayol. *The Practice of Everyday Life*, vol. 2. Minneapolis: University of Minnesota Press, 1998.

Duquoc, Christian and Gustavo Gutiérrez, eds. "Mysticism and the Institutional Crisis." *Concilium* 4 (1994): 17–26.

Dyckman, Katherine, Mary Gavin, and Elizabeth Liebert. *The Spiritual Exercises Reclaimed: Uncovering Liberating Possibilities for Women*. Mahwah, NJ: Paulist Press, 2001.

Eco, Umberto. *On Beauty: A History of a Western Idea*. London: Secker & Warburg, 2004.

Egan, Harvey. *Ignatius the Mystic*. Wilmington, DE: Michael Glazier, 1987.

Evans, G. R., ed. *Bernard of Clairvaux: Selected Works*. Mahwah, NJ: Paulist Press, 1987.

Farley, E. *Faith and Beauty: A Theological Aesthetic*. Aldershot: Ashgate, 2001.

Frances Teresa. *Living the Incarnation: Praying with Francis and Clare of Assisi*. London: Darton, Longman & Todd, 1993.

Galilea, Segundo. "The Spirituality of Liberation." *The Way: A Review of Christian Spirituality* (July 1985): 186–94.

Gibran, Kahlil. *The Prophet*. New York: Alfred A. Knopf, 2019.

Green, Arthur, ed. *Jewish Spirituality*, 2 vols. New York: Crossroad, 1987.

Gutiérrez, Gustavo. *On Job: God-Talk and the Suffering of the Innocent*. Maryknoll, NY: Orbis Books, 1987.

Gutiérrez, Gustavo. *A Theology of Liberation*. Maryknoll, NY: Orbis Books, 1973.

Gutiérrez, Gustavo. *We Drink from Our Own Wells: The Spiritual Journey of a People*. Maryknoll, NY: Orbis Books, 2003.

Hall, B. and D. Jaspers, eds. *Art and the Spiritual*. Sunderland: Sunderland University Press, 2003.

Hall, John N., ed. *George Herbert—The Country Parson; The Temple*. Mahwah, NJ: Paulist Press, 1981.

Hammarskjöld, Dag. *Markings*. London: Faber, 1966.

Hart, Columba, ed. *Hadewijch: The Complete Works*. Mahwah, NJ: Paulist Press, 1980.

Hillesum, Etty. *An Interrupted Life*. New York: Washington Square Press, 1985.

Hossain Nasr, Seyyed, ed. *Islamic Spirituality*, 2 vols. New York: Crossroad, 1991.

Hughes, Gerard J. *Aristotle on Ethics*. London: Routledge, 2001.

Hurlstone Jackson, K., ed. *A Celtic Miscellany*. London: Penguin, 1971.

Imhof, P. and H. Biallowans, eds. *Karl Rahner in Dialogue*. New York: Crossroad, 1986.

Inge, Denise. *Happiness and Holiness: Thomas Traherne and His Writings*. Norwich: Canterbury Press, 2008.

Inge, Denise. *Wanting Like a God: Desire and Freedom in Thomas Traherne*. London: SCM Press, 2009.

Jamal, Mahmood, ed. *Islamic Mystical Poetry: Sufi Verse from the Early Mystics to Rumi*. London: Penguin, 2009.

James, William. *The Varieties of Religious Experience*. New York: Classic Books International, 2010.

Jantzen, Grace. *Power, Gender, and Christian Mysticism*. Cambridge: Cambridge University Press, 1995.

Jones, Kathleen, ed. *The Poems of St John of the Cross*. Tunbridge Wells: Burns & Oates, 1993.

Katz, Steven, ed. *Mysticism and Language*. Oxford: Oxford University Press, 1992.

Katz, Steven, ed. *Mysticism and Philosophical Analysis*. Oxford: Oxford University Press, 1978.

Kavanaugh, Kieran, ed. *John of the Cross: Selected Writings*. Classics of Western Spirituality. New York: Paulist Press, 1987.

Kavanaugh, Kieran, and Otilio Rodriguez, eds. *The Collected Works of St. John of the Cross*. Washington, DC: Institute of Carmelite Studies, 1979.

Kavanaugh, Kieran, and Otilio Rodriguez, eds. *Teresa of Avila: The Interior Castle*. Mahwah, NJ: Paulist Press, 1979.

Lane, Belden. *The Solace of Fierce Landscapes: Exploring Desert and Mountain Spirituality*. New York: Oxford University Press, 1998.

Lonsdale, David. *Eyes to See, Ears to Hear: An Introduction to Ignatian Spirituality*, rev. ed. Maryknoll, NY: Orbis Books, 2000.

Lossky, Vladimir. *The Mystical Theology of the Eastern Church*, rev. ed. London: James Clarke, 1991.

Louth, Andrew. *Denys the Areopagite*. London: Chapman, 1989.

Louth, Andrew. *The Origins of the Christian Mystical Tradition*. Oxford: Oxford University Press, 1981.

Luibheid, Colm. *John Cassian: Conferences*. Mahwah, NJ: Paulist Press, 1985.

Luibheid, Colm. *John Climacus: The Ladder of Divine Ascent*. Mahwah, NJ: Paulist Press, 1982.

Luibheid, Colm, and Paul Rorem, eds. *Pseudo-Dionysius: The Complete Works.* Mahwah, NJ: Paulist Press, 1987.

Malherbe, Abraham J., ed. *Gregory of Nyssa: The Life of Moses.* Mahwah, NJ: Paulist Press, 1978.

Marion, Jean-Luc. *God without Being.* Chicago: Chicago University Press, 1995.

Markus, Robert A. *The End of Ancient Christianity.* Cambridge: Cambridge University Press, 1998.

Martin, Thomas. *Our Restless Heart: The Augustinian Tradition.* London: Darton, Longman & Todd, 2003.

Martinez, Gaspar. *Confronting the Mystery of God: Political, Liberation, and Public Theologies.* New York: Continuum, 2001.

McGinn, Bernard, ed. *Meister Eckhart: Teacher and Preacher.* Mahwah, NJ: Paulist Press, 1986.

McGinn, Bernard, and Edmund Colledge, eds. *Meister Eckhart: The Essential Sermons, Commentaries, Treatises and Defense.* Classics of Western Spirituality. Mahwah, NJ: Paulist Press, 1985.

McGuckin, John. *Standing in God's Holy Fore: The Byzantine Tradition.* London: Darton, Longman & Todd, 2001.

Meyendorff, John. *Byzantine Theology.* New York: Fordham University Press, 1973.

Meyendorff, John, ed. *Gregory Palamas: The Triads.* Mahwah, NJ: Paulist Press, 1983.

Moltmann, Jürgen. *Experiences of God.* Philadelphia: Fortress Press, 1980.

Munitiz, Joseph, and Philip Endean, eds. *Saint Ignatius of Loyola: Personal Writings.* London: Penguin Classics, 2004.

Murk-Jansen, Saskia. *Brides in the Desert: The Spirituality of the Beguines.* Maryknoll, NY: Orbis Books, 1998.

Noffke, Susan, ed. *Catherine of Siena: The Dialogue.* Mahwah, NJ: Paulist Press, 1980.

Nuth, Joan M. *God's Lovers in an Age of Anxiety: The Medieval English Mystics.* London: Darton, Longman & Todd, 2001.

Oliver, Paul. *Mysticism: A Guide for the Perplexed.* London: Bloomsbury, 2009.

Patton, Laurie, ed. *The Bhagavad Gita.* London: Penguin Classics, 2008.

Pelikan, Jaroslav. *Christianity and Classical Culture.* New Haven: Yale University Press, 1993.

Phillips, Catherine, ed., *Mortal Beauty, God's Grace.* Oxford: Oxford University Press, 1986.

Rahner, Hugo. *Ignatius the Theologian.* San Francisco: Ignatius Press, 1990.

Rahner, Karl. "Art against the Horizon of Theology and Piety," 162–68. In *Theological Investigations,* vol. 23. London: Darton, Longman & Todd, 1992.

Rahner, Karl. "Christian Living Formerly and Today," 3–24. In *Theological Investigations,* vol. 7. New York: Herder & Herder, 1971.

Rahner, Karl. "The Theology of Mysticism." In *The Practice of Faith: A Handbook of Contemporary Spirituality.* Edited by K. Lehmann and L. Raffelt, 70–77. New York: Crossroad, 1986.

Ruffing, Janet, ed. *Mysticism and Social Transformation.* Syracuse, NY: Syracuse University Press, 2001.

Schimmel, Annemarie. *Mystical Dimensions of Islam.* Chapel Hill: University of North Carolina Press, 1983.

Schwanda, Tom. *Soul Recreation: The Contemplative-Mystical Piety of Puritanism.* Eugene, OR: Wipf & Stock, 2012.

Sharma, Arvind. *A Guide to Hindu Spirituality.* Bloomington, IN: World Wisdom, 2006.

Sheldrake, Philip. *Heaven in Ordinary: George Herbert and His Writings.* Norwich: Canterbury Press, 2009.

Sheldrake, Philip. *Julian of Norwich: In God's Sight. Her Theology in Context.* Hoboken, NJ: Wiley Blackwell, 2019.

Sheldrake, Philip. *Living Between Worlds: Place and Journey in Celtic Spirituality.* London: Darton, Longman & Todd; Cambridge, MA: Cowley Publications, 1996.

Sheldrake, Philip. *Spaces for the Sacred: Place, Memory and Identity.* London: SCM Press, 2001.

Sheldrake, Philip. *Spirituality: A Guide for the Perplexed.* London: Bloomsbury, 2014.

Sheldrake, Philip. *Spirituality: A Very Short Introduction.* Oxford: Oxford University Press, 2012.

Sheldrake, Philip. *Spirituality and Theology: Christian Living and the Doctrine of God.* London: Darton, Longman & Todd, 1998.

Sheldrake, Philip. *The Spiritual City: Theology, Spirituality, and the Urban*. Hoboken, NJ: Wiley Blackwell, 2014.

Sheldrake, Philip. *The Spiritual Way: Classic Traditions and Contemporary Practice*. Collegeville, MN: Liturgical Press, 2019.

Smelik, Klaas A. D., ed. *Etty: The Letters and Diaries of Etty Hillesum, 1941–1943*. Grand Rapids, MI: Eerdmans, 2002.

Smith, Luther E., Jr. *Howard Thurman: Essential Writings*. Maryknoll, NY: Orbis Books, 2006.

Smith, Luther E., Jr. *Howard Thurman: The Mystic as Prophet*. 3rd ed. Richmond, IN: Friends United Press, 2007.

Sölle, Dorothee. *The Silent Cry: Mysticism and Resistance*. Minneapolis: Fortress Press, 2001.

Spearing, Elizabeth, ed. *Julian of Norwich: Revelations of Divine Love*. London: Penguin Classics, 1998.

Thich Nhat Hanh. *Being Peace*. Berkeley CA: Parallax, 1987.

Thich Nhat Hanh. *Teachings on Love*. Berkeley CA: Parallax, 1998.

Tobin, Frank, ed. *Henry Suso: The Exemplar, with Two German Sermons*. Mahwah, NJ: Paulist Press, 1989.

Tracy, David. *The Analogical Imagination: Christian Theology and the Culture of Pluralism*. New York: Crossroad, 1991.

Tracy, David. *On Naming the Present: God, Hermeneutics and Church*. Maryknoll, NY: Orbis Books, 1994.

Traherne, Thomas. *Centuries*. London: Mowbray, 1975.

Traherne, Thomas. *Selected Poems and Prose*. London: Penguin, 1991.

Turner, Denys. *The Darkness of God: Negativity in Christian Mysticism*. Cambridge: Cambridge University Press, 1995.

Underhill, Evelyn. *Mysticism: The Nature and Development of Spiritual Consciousness*. 1930; repr., London: Oneworld Publications, 1993.

Van Engen, John, ed. *Devotio Moderna: Basic Writings*. Mahwah, NJ: Paulist Press, 1988.

Viladesan, R. *Theological Aesthetics: God in Imagination, Beauty, and Art*. Oxford: Oxford University Press, 1999.

Walker, G. S. M., ed. *Sancti Columbani Opera*. Dublin: 1970.

Ward, Benedicta, ed. *The Desert Fathers: Sayings of the Early Christian Monks*. London: Penguin, 2003.

Ward, Graham, ed. *The Certeau Reader*. Oxford: Blackwell, 2000.

Williams, Rowan. *Teresa of Avila*. London: Geoffrey Chapman, 1991.

Williams, Rowan. "The Via Negativa and the Foundations of Theology: An Introduction to the Thought of V. N. Lossky." In *New Studies in Theology*, vol. 1. Edited by Stephen Sykes and Derek Holmes. London: Duckworth, 1980.

Williams, Thomas, ed. *The Cambridge Companion to Duns Scotus*. Cambridge: Cambridge University Press, 2002.

Windeatt, Barry, ed. *Julian of Norwich: Revelations of Divine Love*. Oxford: Oxford University Press, 2015.

Wiseman, James, ed. *John Ruusbroec: The Spiritual Espousals and Other Works*. Mahwah, NJ: Paulist, 1985.

Woods, Richard, ed. *Understanding Mysticism*. London: Athlone Press, 1981.

Yoshinori, Takeuchi, ed. *Buddhist Spirituality: Indian, Southeast Asian, Tibetan, Early Chinese*. New York: Crossroad, 1995.

Yoshinori, Takeuchi, ed. *Buddhist Spirituality: Later China, Korea, Japan, and the Modern World*. New York: Crossroad, 1999.

INDEX